Where the Game
Matters Most

Also by William Gildea

When the Colts Belonged to Baltimore:
A Father and a Son, a Team and a Time

A Last Championship Season
in Indiana High School
Basketball

Where the Game
Matters Most

William Gildea

Little, Brown and Company

Boston New York Toronto London

First Edition

Map by Brad Wye

The author is grateful for permission to include the following previously copyrighted material: Excerpt from "Last Chance for a Miracle" from the Cincinnati Enquirer. Reprinted by permission of the Cincinnati Enquirer / John Erardi.

Library of Congress Cataloging-in-Publication Data

Gildea, William.
    Where the game matters most : a last championship season in
Indiana high school basketball / William Gildea. — 1st ed.
        p.   cm.

    ISBN 0-316-51967-7
    1. Basketball — Indiana.   2. School sports — Indiana.   I. Title.
GV885.72.I6G55   1997
796.323′63′09772—dc21   97-27491

10 9 8 7 6 5 4 3 2 1

MV-NY
Published simultaneously in Canada by Little, Brown & Company (Canada) Limited

Printed in the United States of America

For Mary Fran

Contents

Acknowledgments

I wish to thank my editors at the *Washington Post*, Len Downie and George Solomon, for granting me a leave of absence from the paper so that I could spend the winter of 1996–97 in Indiana working on this book. Only the extraordinary support of my family and many others enabled me to see it through. I am grateful, above all, to my wife, Mary Fran, for constant encouragement and generosity at every turn, and to Kelly and Billy, David, Maria, and Ann, who made me feel good because they cared so much. I am indebted to Frank Ahrens, David Coen, Jason Crowe, John Feinstein, Faith Hamlin, Paul Hendrickson, Ann Mehlbaum, Michael Pietsch, Tony Reid, and Paul Richard. To all the Hoosiers I met, especially coaches, players, and families, my deepest thanks for your welcome.

Where the Game
Matters Most

Prologue:
Two Shots

March 21, 1954. It's the final huddle, eighteen seconds remaining in the Indiana high school basketball championship game. Little Milan — pronounced MY-lun — has battled powerful Muncie Central to a tie. Milan has the ball. The coach needs a shooter. He looks up confidently at the farm kid named Bobby Plump. The kid has played a mediocre game, but he's the one who led them all season. The plan is made: the ball will be thrown in to Plump and he will go one-on-one against his Muncie defender.

The team's center speaks up. He and the three others should set up a "picket fence" on the left side of the court to lure the defense and give Plump almost the whole floor to work with. "Let's do that," says the coach. Plump will drive to the right and beat his man to the basket for a layup, or pull up and take the jump shot he learned as a boy on winter's frozen earth in southeastern Indiana.

Time in. Plump forgets the start of the play — by mistake, he throws the ball inbounds. But his backcourt partner returns the pass. The game is in Plump's hands. His teammates clear out. The slender boy with the crew cut in the black uniform with black knee-high socks dribbles out deep into the middle of the court. The seconds tick down. Seven, six, five . . .

Plump fakes left and drives right as he has done countless times in front of the backboard nailed to the family smokehouse. At precisely the right end of the free-throw line he stops, jumps, and shoots. The ball rips through the net. It's 32–30 in favor of Milan. The final seconds expire. Milan is champion of all Indiana.

The next day almost 40,000 people descend on Milan, a town of 1,500, to celebrate the victory. People have to park their cars and walk into town. Walk they do, to celebrate what would remain the most famous upset in the history of the sport in Indiana — and the shot that would be lodged in the forever-present of Indiana basketball.

Fast-forward almost forty-three years.

January 23, 1997. Plump is taking another shot. It's an unlikely arena, a gilded conference room on the third floor of the Indiana statehouse in downtown Indianapolis. Two massive chandeliers hang from the high ceiling of the corner room. An Indianapolis insurance agent and restaurateur, Plump is seated in a red leather chair across a thick oak table from a five-foot-four legislator who can block a bill that Plump has inspired. Plump is trying to save the structure of Indiana high school basketball as it has existed for almost a century. Time is running out.

Plump is urging the lawmakers to delay implementation of a decision by the Indiana High School Athletic Association to break up single-class basketball and place Indiana's 382 high schools into four classes based on enrollment, each class with its own tournament at the end of the regular season. The IHSAA's action, which would eliminate the potential drama of small schools upsetting big schools as Milan did in '54, is scheduled to go into effect with the 1997–98 season. Plump wants a bill passed to put off the action so that Indiana voters can express their opinion in a nonbinding referendum. A shy boy who barely managed words after confecting Milan's victory, Plump has grown more outgoing with age. At sixty-two he is still slender, but his sandy hair has gone gray and he's had a double bypass. Now his face is flushed. Pleading for reason, he is impassioned.

"Let's have an informed decision on this, instead of an emotional decision," he says. "We feel that there's not enough information, any information, frankly. We're concerned about the financial impact. It's supposed to be that this is a philosophical decision; well, it's hard to run a program on philosophy. We think the people of Indiana ought to have a vote, where the people will have a chance to preserve the heritage and history of the number one basketball tournament in the United States and the world.

"The state spends all kinds of time and effort sprucing up and taking care of the Soldiers and Sailors Monument in downtown Indianapolis and the George Rogers Clark Memorial in Vincennes. So I don't see why the state can't get involved in something of as much significance as our state basketball tournament. It's about as Hoosier as you can get."

The rules committee chairman suggests that perhaps the General Assembly should not interfere in the decision of a private organization such as the governing body for Indiana high school sports. But he pledges to allow a committee vote on House Bill 1318 and adjourns the hearing.

Plump's last shot hangs in the air.

1

The Mystique

INDIANA. The state is shaped something like a stocking hung on a fireplace at Christmas. Evansville is in the toe. The capital, Indianapolis, is dead center. From it radiate routes to flat fertile farmland, to middle-size cities like Fort Wayne and Kokomo, to the industrial northwest Gary region, which faces Chicago and operates on central time, south to Kentucky and Daniel Boone country. Indiana's hills that parallel the north bank of the Ohio River roll like gentle waves, and the sun sets so slowly on late-autumn days it seems suspended.

Basketball in Indiana, particularly high school basketball, is as universal as the freight whistle there. The game binds diverse people and places. They're all Hoosiers, a term that defies derivation but may stem from a slang expression — "Who's here?" is one of countless possible etymologies. The Hoosier poet James Whitcomb Riley suggested the word derived from a pioneer settler entering a barroom the morning after a brawl, seeing an ear on the floor, and asking, "Whose ear?"

Hoosiers carry on enduring loves. A small display on a desk in the athletic department at Evansville Bosse High defined a Hoosier this way: "A person born or living in Indiana, industrious, hospitable, down-home folk, who enjoys popcorn, race cars and BASKETBALL." And basketball begins in earnest in the high school gyms. The gymnasiums range from the second-floor bandbox of Cannelton High, on the Ohio River, enrollment eighty, to the one at New Castle in eastern Indiana, which seats 9,314 and is the world's largest high school gymnasium. Indiana boasts fifteen of the country's sixteen largest high school gyms. These are known as "Hoosier temples."

Nicholas C. McKay, a protégé of James Naismith, basketball's inventor, brought the game to Indiana in 1893, to Crawfordsville, an early cultural center called the "Athens of Indiana." Crawfordsville's high school teams are still known as the Athenians. Delphi has its Oracles, Martinsville the Artesians, for the spring waters that flowed there. Speedway High is the Sparkplugs. Many teams are called Indians, for whom the state was named; prehistoric Mound Builders of a thousand years ago are the earliest known inhabitants. Elsewhere in the United States basketball was a diversion to fill time between autumn and spring. Not in Indiana. Winter was the one season when rural Hoosiers had free time. The rest was taken up by farming: planting in spring, working the fields in summer, harvesting in fall. As Indiana University coach Bob Knight put it: "Basketball was invented in Massachusetts and developed in Indiana."

The first all-comers high school tournament was held in 1911. Crawfordsville won the championship by beating Lebanon, 24–17. The high school tournament became an annual rite, a sacred institution, a touchstone of Indiana culture. On old recordings, the moment in 1954 when Plump won the state championship for Milan in Indianapolis's Butler Fieldhouse sounds like 15,000 people screaming into the same tin cup. Plump's shot completed an improbable journey through the tournament by a school with only 161 students, a dot on the map. The tournament, open to all schools regardless of size, became the Hoosiers' vehicle for re-enacting the biblical story of David and Goliath.

Nothing like Milan's upset has happened since. But high school basketball and its tournament retained a grip on the Indiana populace. From early legends such as John Wooden of Martinsville's 1927 champions to the latest rising star, Indiana hoops has connected different eras into a strand of brightly burning lights.

There was "The Big O." As Cyril Birge, eighty-one, who jumped center (after every basket) for Jasper in the 1930s and later refereed, said: "As many games as I officiated and watched, you see a lot of people you don't remember. And others, like Oscar Robertson, hell, when he was a sophomore or junior in high school and I saw him I came home and told my wife, 'If there's a better ballplayer than Oscar Robertson, it'd have to be Jesus Christ himself.'"

In 1955 and '56, Robertson led Crispus Attucks of Indianapolis to state championships. The year 1955 marked the first time that an Indianapolis school won the title, and 1956 was the first time that a school in the state went undefeated. Attucks compiled a 61–1 record during Robertson's junior and senior years. The balance of basketball power began to shift to the big-city schools. It was a victory of urban over rural, just as John F. Kennedy's succeeding Eisenhower in 1960 was portrayed by Norman Mailer.

Lebanon's Rick Mount, "The Rocket," with the mid-sixties blond curlicue forelock, was Indiana's "Mr. Basketball" of 1966 and the first high school athlete to look out at America from a *Sports Illustrated* cover. And inside the February 14, 1966, magazine he was pictured wearing narrow-cut jeans and varsity jacket, leaning against a light pole on Main Street. Frank Deford wrote: "Rick Mount does fish for crappies and channel cat out in Cool Lake, and he wanders through the woods outside of town hunting for rabbits with his beagle Bootsy at his side, but he also has a lavender '57 Chevy convertible and a pretty little blonde who wants to be a dental technician, and he takes her to the Sky Vue Drive-In and to the Tom Boy for Cokes and 19-cent hamburgers.''

The seventies brought the reserved Larry Bird, the self-proclaimed "Hick from French Lick," Indiana's ultimate small-town basketball success story: the immortal Boston Celtic. During the eighties, Steve Alford played for his father, Sam, at New Castle, and every time he did, the mammoth field house was filled. Damon Bailey, the state's all-time leading scorer, was loved so much that on March 24, 1990, a crowd of 41,046, the largest ever to attend a high school basketball game, poured into Indianapolis's domed stadium to watch him lead Bedford North Lawrence to the state championship. On the day Bailey delivered the title, the excitement in Indiana was so all-encompassing that the single-class tournament seemed like the Hoosiers' version of soccer's World Cup.

The winnowing process leading to a single champion in Indiana was harrowing. One defeat and a team was out. The 382 teams began play with either two or three sectional games at 64 sites, followed by 16 regionals of 64 teams, then four so-called semistates of four teams each, and finally the final four. To prevail, the champion not only had to escape sectional week and its rivals waiting in ambush but also had to win two games on each of three consecutive Saturdays in the regionals, semistates, and finals. How could most teams think of winning it all?

Indiana traditionalists have always contended that winning the four-week tournament wasn't the important thing. It was everyone having a chance, in theory at least. It was the competing, and the coping with adversity. Most considered the tournament as the chance for modest success, for players to be champions among people who knew them, rather than the champions to thousands they didn't know. The tournament's first stage, the sectionals, crowned the best team in the neighborhood, and offered miracles in doing so. Crossroads Davids would again beat county-seat Goliaths in 1997.

But the 1996–97 high school basketball season in Indiana was like no other this century. There'd been tremors, but the change hit like an earthquake. A way of life was disappearing. The season would be the last in which every one of Indiana's high schools would be grouped together to compete for a single state championship. Before the season even opened, Indianans lamented that the champion to be crowned in the RCA Dome on March 22, 1997, would be what they were calling the last "true" champion. Only three other states — Delaware, Hawaii, and Kentucky — retain single tournaments. The prospect of change so drastic fell heavily on Hoosier hearts.

On April 29, 1996, the Indiana High School Athletic Association's board of directors voted twelve to five to change Indiana's game — a change that, according to polls, was something unwanted by a majority of fans, coaches, and, significantly, athletes. The impetus came from small-school principals who wanted their students to have a better chance to win a title of some sort. In September of that year, Indiana school principals affirmed the board's action by a vote of 220 to 157. Small-school principals again made the difference, although Milan and other small schools voted to keep the tradition. But newer principals and many elected recently to the IHSAA board no longer were so-called "basketball people"; in decades past many school principals were former basketball coaches. In January 1995, a diehard traditionalist retired as the IHSAA commissioner, clearing the way for a vote by the board. The new commissioner, Bob Gardner, was not swayed by sentimentality, even though he once was Milan's principal and a piece of the old Milan gym floor decorated his office.

No less a guardian of Indiana basketball and its traditions than Bob Knight concurred with the move to the class system. "Basketball's changed a lot in twenty or twenty-five years, and there probably are, with certain rare exceptions, only a certain percentage of schools that can actually win a state tournament in a state like this," he said one day after an I.U. practice in Bloomington. "And in the majority of cases, probably the vast majority of cases, they're going to be schools from relatively populated areas. I think a class system provides teams and communities the opportunity to be playing for a state championship where obviously they otherwise wouldn't be. I think people will kind of enjoy the competition that involves relatively equal schools."

Knight had won more than 700 games at I.U., but most Hoosiers disagreed with him on class basketball. When his viewpoint was noted, some even countered that he grew up in Ohio.

Most Hoosiers insisted that, win or lose, little schools taking on bigger ones often motivated young people to do better than they believed possible. Hoosiers argued that at that special time in their lives when almost anything seemed possible, young people were having possibility taken from them.

Bird shared that opinion. "Being from a small town, I really don't like class basketball. My dream and my goal was to play with the big boys, and the only way we could do that was to work our way through the tournament," he said. "Playing against the big boys and beating them is a dream for everyone."

Walking into a high school gym in Indiana in the fall of 1996 meant hearing talk about the demise of the single tournament. Steve Witty, the respected coach of Ben Davis High in Indianapolis, envisioned a serious loss in revenue that went to all the schools' athletic departments, enabling them to operate without taxpayers' money. He foresaw players having to travel farther to tournament games and missing more school time. As coach of a powerhouse team that had won the state championship in 1995 and '96 he admitted that his words had been ridiculed.

"As parents we want our kids to have it better than we had it," said Witty. "What we do is make it easier for them. We want to win the title and we want the media gratification. We're all greedy, we have that quality in our society. But we use basketball to teach the game of life, and when you go to class basketball I don't know what you're teaching kids. Are we teaching them that they're not good enough to go to Indianapolis and take on the big boys? Once there was a group of thirteen colonies. People said they were crazy to take on the most powerful country in the world. If we had a class-basketball mentality back then we might not have our independence today. Now that may be an exaggeration, but life is not a level playing field."

One more thing: "The mystique of Indiana basketball will be lost."

2

Expectations

F OUR TEAMS promised to be genuinely distinctive in the 1996–97 season. One was Anderson, in central Indiana, whose coach was struggling heroically to beat the clock and return to work despite having undergone a liver transplant. Another was Batesville, from the southeastern part of the state, a relatively small school of 589 students hopeful of becoming the modern-day Milan, attuned to the 1954 "miracle" because Milan was just thirteen miles away. A third was DeKalb, located on northeastern Indiana farmland, where a player of immense natural ability named Luke Recker had grown up, the newest in the pantheon of Indiana legends. Finally, there was Merrillville, the 1995 state runner-up that still had its star player and a cause: it came from the Calumet region, or "The Region," the removed industrial upper Northwest area, named for the Calumet River, that was still battling for recognition from the

rest of the state. At the 1995 final four in Indianapolis, the pla-
card affixed to Merrillville's locker-room door was misspelled
"Merriville."

Expectations in Batesville were as high as anywhere in Indiana.
Patrons of the Dairy Queen could talk of little else but the dam-
nable vote and the beautiful Michael Menser, the little shot maker
and soul of the Batesville Bulldogs. Batesville's followers knew it
would take miracle after miracle for a school of its size to win the
state championship. But people in the town of 5,000 believed.
Michael Menser exhilarated Batesville's fans, who considered their
team the last best hope for a small school.

Menser personified Batesville. He played — and played extraor-
dinarily well — against comparative giants. Pale and skinny,
Menser had grown to five foot eleven but he was a wisp at 145
pounds. "Menser," said Jason Crowe, executive director of the
Indiana Basketball Hall of Fame, "is the ultimate Indiana gym rat."
Menser was the self-made country kid who had been dribbling
and shooting a basketball since he could stand up. He'd developed
a knack for shooting at critical times in games as if he were popping jumpers at his backyard hoop in summer; seventeen times
during the 1995–96 season he'd made a shot at the buzzer ending
a game, a half, or a quarter. During a practice in the Batesville
gym, he dribbled between his legs and behind his back as if he
controlled the ball on a string. He shook his head slightly in disgust
when he missed a shot — he expected to make *every* one, even in
practice. Milan was a town of memories, but Menser made Batesville a town of dreams.

But Michael Menser was not the most celebrated of Indiana high
school players going into the 1996–97 season. That distinction
belonged to a bigger, stronger player north of Fort Wayne. Ordi-
narily, DeKalb High, a school of about thirteen hundred located
between Waterloo and Auburn, wouldn't be a contender for a state
championship. But Luke Recker lived in the DeKalb school district.
Recker was so rare a talent that Bob Knight elicited a promise from

him as early as spring following his sophomore season of high school that he would play at Indiana University beginning in the fall of 1997. It was the earliest commitment Knight had ever received from a player.

Recker was a kind of Indiana high school poster boy. He had close-cropped brown hair parted in the middle, tanned skin year-round, an easy smile. "I'm glad you're writing about DeKalb," he said to a visitor on introduction by his coach, a short energetic man named Cliff Hawkins. Recker was personable and already adept at interviews, having conducted them at prestigious basketball camps across the country. In the summer of 1996 the six-five-and-a-half, 195-pounder had certified his talents at camps in Pennsylvania, Indiana, and Las Vegas. He drove for the basket with a jump-start first step, he passed, he scrapped for loose balls, he jumped higher than taller players, he played significant intervals of games with his hands above the rim. He could play any position. He was DeKalb's point guard, but in college he probably would be a perimeter shooting guard. He also was adept at small forward. Most remarkably, perhaps, Recker had been playing as if unperturbed by personal turmoil. Although his senior season should have been a time of pure joy, Recker's parents were divorcing. His father worked in Iowa. His mother maintained the Recker home in a neighborhood called "The Village of Duesenberg" in Auburn. Auburn, Indiana, once was the home of E. L. Cord, the innovative carmaker of the thirties who produced the Auburn, the Cord, and the Duesenberg. Now Auburn was known in Indiana as the home of Luke Recker. He was the new "Duesy."

Jamaal Davis began the season as one of Recker's main rivals for the state's coveted title of "Mr. Basketball." Boys grow up in Indiana dreaming of becoming "Mr. Basketball" as girls dream of becoming "Miss America." "Mr. Basketball" gets to wear the coveted number 1 jersey for the Indiana high school all-stars in an annual two-game series for seniors against Kentucky's best each

June. In Indiana a "Mr. Basketball" is never forgotten. Like Recker, Davis possessed the skills to turn a reasonably good team into a title contender. The six-eight, 205-pound Davis played for Merrillville, eight miles south of crime-torn Gary. Davis lived in Gary with his mother before moving to his father's house in Merrillville; his parents had been divorced and remarried. The Davises, father and son, were among many African-Americans moving from Gary to Merrillville. Merrillville High was a predominantly white school of 2,000 students, but in recent years black enrollment had grown from close to zero to about 15 percent. Davis encountered a difficult adjustment to the harder curriculum, but he persevered. Still, if Batesville's Menser and DeKalb's Recker suggested the Indiana of the imagination — schoolboys shooting backyard baskets under a glinting sunlight in the country's peaceful heart — Merrillville's Davis embodied harsher realities in Indiana life and basketball.

One Saturday morning in the Merrillville gym, Davis sat in the stands and related stories of his years in Gary that left the impression that he was blessed to have reached the age of seventeen. He said that gangs and drugs had killed a number of people he knew and loved, including a friend who recently had been riddled by bullets. As a freshman Davis had been ruled ineligible to play the first thirteen games because of poor grades. As a junior he had been suspended for two games for arguing with his coach. At the start of his senior season more controversy roiled. A newspaper reported that illegal phone calls had been made by Purdue to the Davis family before Jamaal had signed a letter of intent to enroll at the school. Before that, Purdue had penalized an assistant coach for giving Davis a ride during a period in which the National Collegiate Athletic Association's rules decreed that college recruiters and high school players were to have no contact. In the midst of the latest furor, Jim East, Merrillville's coach, struggled for Davis's attention. In Davis's sophomore year Merrillville had made it to the state championship game only to lose by a single point. Davis proved then he could be a big-game player, scoring twenty points. Now East wanted Davis to show this Merrillville team the way downstate, to the finals.

In Anderson, a working-class city of about 59,000, located twenty-eight miles northeast of Indianapolis, coach Ron Hecklinski had been grooming an impressive array of players since they graduated from eighth grade. But Anderson High could improve on its previous season's finish among Indiana's top eight teams only if an exceptionally fast five-foot-ten junior point guard named Eric Bush could meet all of Hecklinski's expectations. Bush had to be a team leader. But his life had been defined by reaction and survival, not leadership. His mother died of an asthma attack when she was thirty-nine; his father had done time in jail on a drug charge. An African-American, Bush struggled to adjust when a white couple became his legal guardians. Basketball made him happy — but when Hecklinski's health began to fail in 1996, Bush feared that he'd been fated. With the coach ailing and the season nearing, he felt uncertainty, not confidence.

Besides these four players and their teams there was a mysterious player just arrived in Indianapolis — a "move-in," as Indiana basketball newcomers are called — who was raising expectations. The name had gotten around the city as he and his mother looked for a school for his senior year. They'd come from Danville, Illinois, with a collection of newspaper clippings telling of his basketball skills, people quoted as saying that he was the best around. The move-in's mother made the decision: her son would be attending Indianapolis's North Central, the largest high school in Indiana, with 3,070 students. Doug Mitchell, North Central's coach, envisioned the new player adding the last ingredients for a championship run, "toughness, grit, a willingness to do anything to win." He'd floated into the state as quietly as ground fog, but soon everyone would know his name: Huggy Dye.

3

"Heck"

A TALL man silhouetted by dim light approaches from the end of a long, narrow corridor. He limps. He stops and leans against a wall. At last, coming fully into view, he smiles. "Told you I was moving slow," he says. Forty years old, Ron Hecklinski is tall and handsome, with thick brown hair rippling down his neck and over his collar. But his eyes are deep-hollowed, his complexion starkly pale. A grimace telegraphs pain from somewhere in his frail body, bent like an old man's.

But he insisted on being there in that ancient gymnasium next to the railroad tracks in Anderson, Indiana, even if only two months earlier he had undergone ten and a half critical hours of transplant surgery to receive a new liver. Now it is the last week of October 1996, which means the beginning of basketball practice for most high schools in Indiana. As coach of Anderson High

School, Hecklinski has assembled a team regarded so highly that it is ranked number two in the state in a preseason poll. Anderson has a genuine chance to be the best in the state, a place where it's often said that life is a game and that the game — basketball — is life.

Step by step, Hecklinski made it into his cramped, windowless office and lowered himself gently to the chair behind his desk. Quicker than he could move he professed the opposite of what would soon be obvious: "I'm not going to sacrifice my health for basketball." Two assistant coaches sitting in the room shifted slightly. They knew his intense nature and they could feel his desire to win the state championship. This championship would carry even more significance than usual because it was the last one-class tournament in Indiana history. The winner would be remembered forever. As a result, all Indiana coaches with teams talented enough to win the title — including Hecklinski, ailing or not — viewed the 1996–97 season as a chance to make history as Indiana's "last true champions." Tradition was about to be swept away. Amid disappointment and anger, teams with championship aspirations began practice with passion. It was as if someone had started a clock and time was running out in what had seemed a timeless era.

The phone rang in Hecklinski's office. An assistant coach at New Mexico State was on the line, asking his friend how he was feeling during the first week of practice. Was he physically up to the demands of coaching so soon after a liver transplant? Hecklinski made light of his condition but couldn't camouflage a hoarse voice, a condition made permanent by yelling and already worsened in two days of practice. "The guy whose liver it was was a musician," he said with a laugh, not knowing really who his donor was, "so actually my voice is better."

"Heck" liked to maintain an irreverent tone; he'd always considered himself a tough guy. But sometimes these days he couldn't help lapsing into seriousness. Earnestly, to his friend on the phone, he said, "To know that some young man, a twenty-year-old, died and donated his organs that enabled not only me but four other people to live, what a gift that is. Now I have two birthdays.

"It's so good to be back, to see my kids, who have gotten a year older. They're getting better. It's good for me to see that."

At Anderson High, Hecklinski's surgery and physical condition overshadowed the class basketball controversy. Beneath his green sweatsuit a wavy scar stretched across his stomach from hip to hip, a permanent reminder of the incision and his ordeal. Muscles and tissues and nerves in his abdomen had yet to heal. Sudden moves caused him pain. He lacked stamina. He felt dazed at times from the drugs he had to take. He had trouble moving his left arm. He had regained only partial feeling in the arm that had to be extended back and above his head during the surgery; nerve damage had eliminated the feeling in his thumb and adjoining two fingers. While he could move the arm, mostly he kept it at his side, dangling, the fingers splayed.

Ron Hecklinski grew up in a basketball family, and basketball had everything to do with his life. If it weren't for basketball, he would not have met his wife, Pam. If it weren't for basketball, he might not have had the degree of determination that he needed during his liver transplant. But he might not have been in basketball. He meant to be a dentist.

He came from South Bend. He was born January 6, 1956, one of six children, including four boys, three of whom became coaches. Their father, Joe, and his twin brother, Ernest, played basketball for South Bend Washington when John Wooden coached South Bend Central. Wooden, when asked about the pair during return visits to South Bend, always answered something like: "Oh, yes, I remember those Hecklinski twins — they would give me fits."

The twins played for two years at Indiana University under

Branch McCracken, an earlier Bloomington basketball coaching legend. Then they entered the service during World War II and became dental technicians. After the war, they both attended St. Louis University and became dentists. They operated the same office together in South Bend for forty years. There was one sure way to tell them apart, Ron said. "Dad was a lefty; Uncle Ernest was right-handed."

Ron couldn't pass a college calculus course he needed for predent — as he liked to say, Joe and Ernie would have been a tough act to follow anyway. Ron was an athlete, basketball and baseball his best sports. After graduating from South Bend St. Joseph's in 1974, he accepted a scholarship at St. Edward's University, in Austin, Texas. But the Hoosier came home after only one semester; he transferred to Manchester College, in North Manchester, Indiana, thirty-five miles west of Fort Wayne. There, he made the all-conference basketball team two years and was Manchester's co-captain for two years.

In 1981 he got his first high school coaching job at Wapahani (enrollment 350), in Selma, near Muncie. Tammie Buchanan was one of the basketball players on the girls' team, and Ron happened to notice her older sister during a visit. That was Pam, a student at Ball State, in Muncie. "I had the inside track because I knew Tammie," said Ron. They were married in 1984 in Mooreland, in eastern Indiana, in Buck Creek Church, the same church in which her parents had been married.

They moved around. Jasper High in 1984–85. Edgewood, near Bloomington, from 1986 through 1989. He worked as a college assistant at Illinois State in 1985–86 and for four seasons, 1989–1993, at Ball State. In 1990 Ball State made the NCAA's "sweet sixteen" and played a sensational game against UNLV, losing 69–67, in Oakland, California. Ball State had the ball last but couldn't get off a shot; UNLV went on to win the NCAA championship.

In 1993 Hecklinski applied for the Anderson job because he wanted to locate in one place, and because life on the road scouting games was keeping him from Pam and daughter Stephanie, who was born in 1988. That year everything had seemed right for Ron. Pam was pregnant; his Edgewood Mustangs had just completed a 16–5 season. But then results of a blood test to check his cholesterol showed numbers that suggested a possible liver problem. So did another test taken a few months later. He was tested thoroughly and learned that he had contracted, without apparent reason, a liver disease known as primary sclerosing cholangitis. There was no cure for it.

He was told that eventually he would need a transplant. But after the shock of that news, his life went on just about normally. He thought he wouldn't need the transplant till he was about sixty years old. But he began to feel fatigue and to lose weight toward the end of his stay at Ball State. At Anderson the symptoms continued. During his third season they accelerated dramatically. In public he continued to be his upbeat self; few knew how bad he felt. He'd take midday naps. In the evenings at home he'd all but collapse. His spleen began to enlarge. Varices — weak areas in his veins — developed near his esophagus; he ran the risk of bleeding to death if a vein burst.

He decided to reveal his problem to close friends in case he needed quick help. He told his two main assistant coaches, Terry Turner, who had been on the school's staff since 1986, and a sixty-nine-year-old volunteer assistant, John Wilson — Jumpin' Johnny Wilson, who led Anderson High to its last state championship, in 1946, when he was Indiana's "Mr. Basketball." Wilson played four sports for Anderson College, then toured with the Harlem Globetrotters for five years with the likes of Marques Haynes and Goose Tatum and future New York Knick Nat "Sweetwater" Clifton — "the good years," Wilson called them.

Turner aspired to a head-coaching job, but loved Anderson High so much that he'd stayed longer than he anticipated. Wilson had coached basketball and served as athletic director at Malcolm X College, in Chicago. In 1989 he came home to Anderson and took a job as assistant basketball coach at his alma mater, known now as Anderson University. In 1995 Hecklinski talked Wilson into giving up his paying job at the university for a volunteer job at the high school. Hecklinski was at his persuasive best after getting to know Wilson when Wilson substituted briefly as a gym teacher at the high school. "I think he thought he'd have more fun here," said Hecklinski. "He's always been an Indian."

Hecklinski could have relied heavily on Turner and Wilson during the 1995–96 season, but it had never been in his makeup to ask others for help. "I operated tired," he said. "When you do something you love to do, you do it. On the court, you do your job. When I'd come home, I'd sleep. I shirked home responsibilities. I'd come home and do nothing."

By late summer of 1996, however, Hecklinski knew he would have to delegate authority. He wondered whether he would be able to coach at all. Turner and Wilson assured him they would take care of things. Wilson, a man of few words but with a reputation for well-chosen ones, counseled "Heck" to relax and concentrate on getting well.

At a postseason banquet for the 1995–96 Anderson team, a fan named Mary Porter, who had found out about Hecklinski's illness, offered the coach a suggestion. Her son, Steve, worked for a pharmaceutical company involved in drug research for liver transplant patients. Did Hecklinski mind if she phoned her son and sought his advice? Hecklinski told her he would appreciate it. After Steve Porter showed Ron's medical records to a number of doctors, he called back in alarm. This was a problem that needed immediate action. He recommended that they make an appointment with David H. Van Thiel, medical director of the transplant center at the University of Kentucky Chandler Medical Center.

Ron sensed the urgency. He had been feeling weaker and weaker, and growing jaundiced. Primary sclerosing cholangitis attacks the bile ducts of the liver. Body wastes can build up. In some cases a person can contract cancer — cholangiolar carcinoma. If that already had happened to Hecklinski it was doubtful he could be placed on a transplant list.

At Lexington Ron and Pam met with Van Thiel. It was May 24, 1996. Not as tall as the six-foot-five Hecklinski, Van Thiel nevertheless was a big man with a sense of humor. Hecklinski and Van Thiel liked each other. But the doctor got to business quickly. Moments into a routine endoscopic examination, doctors were stunned. Hecklinski was hemorrhaging. His blood, instead of flowing through his liver, had backed up into his spleen and up into the veins of his esophagus. "It was spontaneous varix bleeding," Van Thiel recalled. "A person has a twenty-five percent chance of dying as a result of that experience. This gave the situation some urgency." Hurriedly, doctors tied off five swollen veins and hospitalized Ron until he stabilized.

He thought: *What if this happened when I was fishing?* Just days before, he had gone far out into Lake Michigan on a charter boat. He had gone partly unaware of how bad his condition was, and partly in denial that he had a serious problem at all. Now doctors were telling him that had he hemorrhaged on the fishing trip, he'd have bled to death by the time the boat could have gotten back to shore.

When he returned to Lexington for a second examination two weeks later doctors tied off four more veins near his stomach. Then they placed him on their liver transplant list — being cancer-free, he qualified — and sent him home to wait. As word of his health got around Anderson, he reassured people: "Everything's going to be all right." It was bravado. He knew the chance of dying while waiting for a new liver was 25 percent. He wondered, *Will I die waiting? Will I die in surgery? Will a transplant fail?* As for coaching the 1996–97 season, that seemed almost impossible. He prayed.

On August 29, Hecklinski got the call from Lexington. "Be here by midnight," the transplant coordinator told him. It was 6:45. It's a three-hour drive from Anderson to Lexington, with an additional hour lost to the clock because Indiana remains on standard time all year. They could make it, although they couldn't dawdle. Neighbors took Stephanie, now eight years old, as Ron and Pam went to gather their things. In the middle of their family room they experienced the full impact of the call. Finally it had come. He was happy about that. But for the first time he was afraid. They held one another tightly, both crying.

"We're going to leave here like we're going on vacation," Pam told Ron. They wanted to leave Stephanie with a good feeling. Pam closed her suitcase. Ron, who hadn't packed because he thought he'd jinx the call from coming, haphazardly scooped up clothes. Pam's parents arrived to move in temporarily and care for Stephanie. Ready to leave, Ron kissed his daughter, hugged her, and smiled, trying to reassure her. At 7:30, he backed his green '94 Ford Explorer out of the garage.

He then took several wrong turns. They'd rehearsed the route. I-69 south to state Route 9 south to I-74 east to Cincinnati to I-75 south to Lexington. Instead, he ended up barreling down state Route 3 toward New Castle. And, Pam noticed, he wasn't driving carefully, passing cars without looking back when he pulled in front of them, his eyes fixed straight ahead. Twenty miles into it she told him to pull over. She drove. He got on his new cell phone and ran up a $412 bill calling friends. He kept all the conversations lighthearted.

"I never really allowed myself to think of being scared beforehand," he said. "I've always been a positive person. I guess it comes from being involved in athletics, and being successful. However, right before the surgery I was *really* frightened, and I could see that this could be it. People die on the table. My wife is the strong one. If it hadn't been for her strength and courage to keep me going, it would have been really, really hard. She helped me think about being there for Stephanie. I couldn't imagine my daughter having to go through life without her dad.

"I remember a nurse telling Pam it was time to say good-bye. She said, 'It's not good-bye. I'll see him in a few hours.' "

The doctors broke two of Ron's ribs so they could lift his rib cage, remove the diseased liver, and implant the good one. During the marathon procedure one of his lungs collapsed. When they were done doctors told Pam that every moment he lived was a triumph. Then every hour and then every day became a triumph. Not that Ron remembers any of his four days in intensive care, or Pam talking softly to him, asking him to squeeze her hand if he heard her, and him squeezing.

When Ron came to and understood where he was and what had happened, he was looking directly into Pam's eyes. He wished he could tell her how much he loved her, tell her over and over. But it hurt even to speak. Basketball? It was days before he thought of it.

Two weeks later he was released from the hospital but had to stay in Lexington to be monitored daily. Pam found a short-term rental apartment. She rented a reclining chair for him to sleep in because he had trouble lying flat.

On October 2 he had to be readmitted to the hospital for treatment of a viral hepatitis. "A serious infection," Van Thiel said. Ron and Pam worried. He still had not reached the six-week hurdle that, according to statistics, would give him an 85 percent chance to live one year. But he responded to the treatment and was released two days later.

Stephanie's grandparents drove her to Lexington twice to see her father, once when he was in the hospital and once at the apartment. Each time Ron laughed and joked enough to reassure her. But even as the October days passed he still suffered severe pain and had trouble standing straight. One day he went for a walk with his father-in-law at a nearby mall. Hunched over and weak, looking this way and that so no one would bump into him, Ron gave the appearance of being disoriented. Two elderly women approached him. "Are you lost, sonny?" one asked.

Another incident startled him. Hecklinski recalled, "At this Pizza Hut, I have to go to the men's room. I'm in there with the door locked; it's taking me forever to get myself together. And this guy is pounding on the door. Finally he yells, 'If you don't come out of there I'm going to punch you out.' When I come out I cover up my midsection in case he hauls off and hits me, and it's this little guy, seventy-five years old. 'Please don't hit me,' I say. I'm serious.''

On Monday, October 28, Pam took Ron home to Anderson.

They reached the city at 2:15 P.M. But he'd gotten her to promise something, and now she would keep that promise. She drove directly to the Anderson High gymnasium and dropped him off. It was the first day of practice. He made it on will.

"I wanted to be here Halloween so I could take my daughter trick-or-treating, and I made it three days early." That's how he put it on Wednesday of the first week of practice. "There's two agendas I still think I have. I've got to help raise Stephanie and make sure she's okay. I've got to work with young kids; I have a lot to offer young kids. But basketball for me is a bonus. I'm not going to sacrifice my own health. In the past I always sacrificed my health, always up watching films late at night. I've got to be efficient; I'm going to do that.''

"It helped him to have a goal — he had a reason to get back, to work," Van Thiel said. "He had a job to do, mobilize the kids. You can't sit around and think.''

Again it was a matter of odds: if Ron could survive a year he had a 90 to 95 percent chance to live five years. Living five years, according to Van Thiel, would put him "probably on a normal survival curve.''

Being busy was good, but he couldn't do too much. Could he restrain himself as he'd promised? Especially during the upcoming season, when the players he loved would have a chance to be state champions? It would be hard, given his personality red-lettered in a single word on the wall behind his desk: Intensity.

"So now I'm reduced to this," he said. He pulled a megaphone from behind his desk. He needed it because he was too weak to shout instructions to his players. He demonstrated with a laugh: "Get up and down the court, you guys. Let's go." He couldn't even stand up during practice but would be confined to a classroom desk placed on the sideline. Holding the megaphone in his good right hand he inched his way around the desk in his office, saying, "You just live day by day, have the best day you can."

He walked slowly along another dim corridor until he stepped out into a cream-colored light streaming from the rafters of the imposing gymnasium. When all the bleachers are lowered, the place holds 8,996 — it's the world's second largest high school gym. The top rows way up in sections XX and YY reach to within arm's length of girders that stretch across a ceiling as high as a large airplane hangar's.

Hecklinski stood bathed in the light, soaking in a peaceful moment. The only sounds were the bouncing of basketballs and the swishing of nets as his players shot around on the floor, which was polished like a dinner table.

He raised his megaphone: "All right, you guys . . ."

4

The Road
to Batesville

WHEN you drive out of a city in Indiana, you reach the country quickly. Flat fields extend to the horizon. Only an occcasional house or barn dots the land. On a late-October day it already looked like winter, gray, with most of the leaves fallen. A CSX freight inched its way west. A FOR SALE sign hung from an abandoned brick building that once was Holton High; on the macadam next to it fresh nets hung from the rims. Signs along the road advised TIME TO WINTERIZE. And, with election day nearing: VOTE FOR WHITEY.

Down a shoulderless road, 300 North, to Milan. A red combine funneled corn, plucked from the cobs, into a blue dump truck. Across an old stone bridge stood the Milan water tower with its dominating inscription: STATE CHAMPS, 1954. Since that year visitors have followed a psychic tug to a town that symbolizes life's improbabilities. As the droll Ron Corfman, sports editor of the neighboring *Versailles* (pronounced "Ver-SALES") *Republican and Osgood Journal*, said: "It's one year that will never end."

Corfman's predecessor was Tiny Hunt, a big man who chronicled Milan's finest days and talked basketball with the crowds at Rosie Arkenberg's restaurant in downtown Milan. Rosie's used to close for the games and reopen afterward and stay open until everyone had their fill. Tiny is long dead and Rosie's "Ideal Dining Room" is closed. Businesses in Milan have shut down over the years — the furniture store, the movie theater. But, among others, Chester Nichols's barbershop, American flag out front, still thrives. Nichols had been cutting hair there since 1948, and his father worked there before him.

Visitors still find Roselyn McKittrick's antiques and collectibles at the corner of Carr and Franklin. Inside the old double doors is a shop of treasures, things wooden with years of gleam on them, and plenty of Milan basketball memorabilia. Books. Tapes of the '54 title game. And stories. McKittrick is the town's unofficial hoops historian.

"We had a couple here recently from Pittsburgh," she said. "I had a letter from New Hampshire. A writer from Cincinnati was here. Another writer in Texas did an article. We have a lot of big older men who used to play — you can just see 'em when they're coming. And coaches. There was this young coach a while back who was starting off his career at Crawfordsville. He said he had heard his dad talking about Milan. You could see the dream in his eyes.

"It's one of those stories that's passed down from fathers to sons. People come and they talk about the David-and-Goliath aspect of what the '54 team did. It's the dream of a small town, to do what they did. It's a feeling that goes deep in all of us — the great upset. The team just kept picking up steam through the tournament, and life then was built around the high school and the team."

One could imagine it, standing on the vacant street outside the

Railroad Inn restaurant as a freight rumbled just a few yards away through the heart of town. Inside the Railroad Inn, the black-and-yellow Milan letter jacket once worn by Gene White, who played center on the '54 team, is displayed in a lighted case. A painting of the team hangs on the wall. The town is just a few hundred larger than it was more than forty years before. It almost seems like 1954.

It surely did out in nearby Pierceville. Turning off Route 350 onto a narrow road, you cross the railroad tracks into the community that produced four of the ten players on the '54 Milan team — White and Bobby Plump and Roger Schroder and Glenn Butte — the "Pierceville Alley Cats," who played in the "alley" behind the Schroder store. The Schroder house is there, but the store is boarded up. White's feed store is gone. Beyond some dead cornstalks is the two-story yellow frame house Plump grew up in; behind it he honed the jump shot that he used to beat Muncie Central for the state title. "You had to be careful not to fall into the manure pile near the basket," said Plump.

"We were like brothers," recalled Butte, a big man with glasses and gray hair, athletic director of Batesville High for twenty-five years before retiring in 1994. "The four of us grew up together. We could see each other's houses. In the summers we'd go fishing and camping on the creek near Versailles. There was hardly a day when we didn't play basketball."

But Milan's memories have been hard on Milan coaches since Marvin Wood, played by Gene Hackman in the 1986 film *Hoosiers*, left after the championship season. No coach has lasted longer than six years. The last winning season was 1988–89. At one stretch Milan went two years without winning a home game. "People told me this is a graveyard for coaches," said Randy Combs, thirty-three, who took his wife, Lisa, and year-old son, Cameron, south in September 1994, after being an assistant coach in the Indianapolis suburb of Greenfield, a place of poetry and basketball, which in Indiana is practically the same thing. Greenfield is a launching

pad for coaches and the birthplace of Hoosier poet James Whitcomb Riley, who wrote of autumn, when basketball begins:

> When the frost is on the punkin and the fodder's
> in the shock
> And you hear the kyouck and gobble of the
> struttin' turkey-cock
> And the rooster's hallylooyer as he tiptoes on the
> fence;
> O, it's then's the times a feller is a-feeling at his
> best,
> With the risin' sun to greet him from a night of
> peaceful rest,
> As he leaves the house, bareheaded, and goes out
> to feed the stock,
> When the frost is on the punkin and the fodder's
> in the shock.

Combs left Greenfield to take over a Milan team that had gone
2–18 because, unpromising as the job appeared, Milan was his
chance to become a head coach. He bought a house three blocks
from Milan's new school, a large brick building on the edge of
town, and went to work. Combs knows what it takes to win in
Indiana. He played on a state champion, Vincennes Lincoln, in
1981, and wears a championship ring. At Vincennes Lincoln he
also learned the pressures faced by high school basketball coaches
in Indiana. He told of his old coach, a man named Gunner.

"Gunner Wyman was one of the best," Combs said. "But when
I was a sophomore there was a petition to fire him. He had to go
before the school board. He pleaded that he wanted just two more
years. So his last game, he won the state. He got the last laugh.
He retired and went home to Kentucky. He lives alone out in the
country and raises hunting dogs. And he remembers every name
on that petition."

Combs had to find a way to win if he was either to stay in

Milan or advance to a better coaching job. Modest improvement heartened him. In 1995–96 he nudged the team's record to 5–15, with eleven of the losses decided in the fourth period. One of those games was with Batesville. "We had Batesville beat," he said, "but we made some bad decisions near the end." Batesville may be a small school, but it's bigger than Milan. Milan still is one of the smallest schools in the state even with its enrollment up to 325, double what it was in the everlasting year of 1954. The 1954 championship trophy is still the centerpiece of the school's lobby. The 1954 banner hangs above the basketball court. Combs said that some students were tired of hearing about the '54 team, and produced a newspaper article from February 1996, in which a couple of senior players said they favored multi-class basketball. Combs, an unwavering traditionalist, wasn't unhappy to see those players move on. "In the words of Gunner Wyman," said Combs, "graduation sometimes is a good thing."

Combs intended to keep pointing out to his players the virtues of the team that worked the so-called Milan miracle. "What the '54 team represents is kids coming together for the common goal, blending their talents, sacrificing individually for the good of the team. Let's build on what lessons were taught by that group."

But Combs's father, a doctor in Vincennes, disagreed. "I've got to tell you, Randy, I'm a convert," the father said. "I think class basketball makes sense. After watching Vincennes [Lincoln] take apart South Knox . . . The strength difference was something. By the fourth quarter, South Knox was beat."

"You can only put five on the floor at once," argued the son.

That was popular basketball thinking in Milan, even though Indiana high school football was divided into five classes and Milan made the 1996 final four in the smallest class, providing an infusion of school spirit. But in football, classes by enrollment make sense. A single tournament would take months to play since football is played only once a week. Far more players were needed to field a football team than a basketball team, and clearly larger schools had a greater number of physically capable players — creating a likelihood of lopsided games and injuries. But size of the school doesn't matter nearly as much in basketball. Besides, said Combs, "it's not just winning, it's achieving." He was eager to win in 1996–97, and at least to "achieve" against Batesville. But he imagined that Michael Menser would work some magic. "I hope I have a player to guard him," he said. This season the game would be played in Batesville.

From Combs's house it is just two quick turns to an utterly empty road and a short drive into Batesville. A church steeple leads to a downtown of quiet streets, pristine homes and lawns, and a quaint main square resembling an Old World village. Batesville is a postcard from America's Midwest.

"When I was growing up, like a lot of kids, I couldn't wait to get out," said Melvin Siefert, Batesville High's coach, who looked even younger than his thirty-three years. "After I left I couldn't wait to get back. This is a great place to raise a family. It's a great place to work, with a Fortune 500 company in our backyard." That would be Hillenbrand Industries, which makes caskets and hospital furniture. A hand-lettered sign inside the school's front door warned: JUST BECAUSE HILLENBRAND MAKES CASKETS, YOU DON'T HAVE TO TRY ONE! DON'T DRINK AND DRIVE!

Like the rest of town, it is orderly and spotless out in the wide-open area surrounding the high school, with its address taken from the school's nickname: One Bulldog Boulevard. Siefert's wife, Amy, taught math at Batesville's middle school. Siefert once was Batesville's star quarterback. His photograph, a pose with his arm cocked as if ready to pass the football in his hand, hangs with photos of other former Batesville standouts near an entrance to the gym. The blond hair that covers his ears in the photograph had been clipped burr-short. He'd played football at Butler University, in Indianapolis, and got his first job as an assistant football coach at Batesville. But he was drawn to basketball. "Like a lot of people in this state, I like football," he said, "but I love basketball."

He had made a study of the game. One of his bibles was at hand: *Basketball's Half-Court Offense*, by John Calipari.

To a team with relatively little height, Siefert taught a basic brand of basketball. On offense his players looked as if they were playing in a revolving door; they forever circled, someone always rotating toward the player with the ball. They passed, they picked, they cut, they searched for the easy basket. They epitomized the control, precision, and discipline of Indiana basketball. There was no such thing allowed as a harebrained shot, unless it was taken by Menser, in which case it only looked harebrained momentarily because it was part of his repertoire and usually went in. Defense? Old-fashioned Indiana man-to-man with zone principles that occasionally could be applied — but usually it was chest to opponent's chest, nothing conciliatory. All of that would become apparent in time. For now Siefert walked to an empty classroom and slapped a tape into a VCR. This would show why Milan's Combs was concerned. Siefert fast-forwarded to the final seconds of the final game of the previous season's Ripley County tournament. "Watch this," he said.

South Dearborn grabs a two-point lead and apparent victory with only six seconds remaining. Batesville calls time-out. The tape skips to the inbounds play. The ball comes on deep in the backcourt to Menser. He has almost the length of the floor to cover, moving right to left. He outdistances one defender. Two more opponents drive him toward the near sideline. But he stops as abruptly as a speeding car at the edge of a cliff in a cartoon, dribbles behind his back, and darts between the two opponents. He cuts across midcourt on a diagonal toward the middle of the floor and, thirty feet from the basket, elevates as straight as a pole with his legs tucked behind him. The buzzer goes off. The ball kisses off the backboard and plops through the net for a three-pointer. The Bulldogs win by one. The Batesville play-by-play announcer sounds as if he's going crazy, little Menser disappears under a swarm of teammates, students clamber down out of the stands onto the floor.

"I get goosebumps just watching that," said Siefert. He exuded confidence talking about his Bulldogs. He had one starter who was six feet five, three who were six three, and Menser. They were all brown-haired except for Menser, who had a black crew cut and heavy eyebrows. "I don't know that height is going to be a problem for us," Siefert said. "We're going to get up and down the floor. We have quick kids. Oh, yeah. They're a loose bunch of kids." They played a controlled game but they also loved to run — they could do both, that was the beauty of the Bulldogs. "And they're smart," continued Siefert, "good kids from good families. Michael doesn't make bad decisions on the court. We have the experience — 61–14 the last three years. We've handled pressure." In 1995–96 Batesville went 23–1, including three victories in the tournament sectional, leaving it the smallest of 64 surviving schools headed into the regionals. The regional took place in the cavernous gym at New Castle across a parking lot from the Indiana Basketball Hall of Fame. It was a close game, the kind Menser often had won with a buzzer-beating shot. But in New Castle, Batesville was Menserized.

Playing on its home court, New Castle won the game when its own little guard named Josh Estelle sank a long shot as time ran out. New Castle 62, Batesville 61. The season was over for the Bulldogs. Batesville had come close to making the "sweet sixteen." Siefert didn't care to roll the tape of that defeat because for him the mere thought of it was painfully vivid. "It was amazing how the emotions changed," he said. "You went from euphoric to stunned."

But the defeat did not change his mind about dividing the tournament into separate classes. "At one time I was for the class system," he said. "But the more you think about it, it is special, the one-class system, and we have been able to compete relatively well. You know what winning the state did for those Milan players, their future occupations. They were heroes.

"Just before the summer I wrote the kids a letter. I told them they had a chance to win four sectionals in a row, the opportunity to win four conference championships in a row." He also told them this: "We need to start thinking and dreaming about being the last team to win the state tournament in a single-class system. It can be done with hard work and dedication!"

Was that an impossible dream? It seemed that sooner or later in the tournament Batesville would play a school too big, a team too talented. It seemed too much to imagine that Batesville of 1997 could replicate Milan of 1954, that the last champion of single-class basketball could be a relatively small school.

But Siefert seemed genuine in his belief that Batesville could win it all.

And if he believed, so would his players.

5

Luke and Jamaal

A SEARING spotlight shone on Luke Recker. He was only seventeen years old, and yet he was one of the most talked about people in Indiana. He was the best-known player in Indiana high school basketball going into the 1996–97 season and the most highly touted Indiana high school player in years. The attention on Recker was enormous. This is how it is in Indiana when a youngster is hailed as the next "Mr. Basketball" and has committed to I.U. as a sophomore. Coaches and fans from around the state followed him in person, on radio or television, in the press, on the Internet. Recker appeared eager to take on everything asked of him, which can be a burden to a young person, no matter how willing.

His life seemed perfectly ordered. He lived on a street as pastoral as the name suggests: Golden Hawk Drive. He had a basketball court in his backyard. Attached to the headboard of his bed was

"The Athlete's Prayer": "Lord, please clear my head of all distractions, and my heart of burdens I may bear, so I may perform my very best, knowing You'll always be there." Going into his senior year at DeKalb, Recker ranked ninth out of 315 students in his class. During the summer he had been the most valuable player in the Las Vegas National Tournament, the leading scorer at the Nike All-American Camp in Indianapolis, which brings together the best 100 to 150 high school players in the country, and an all-star for the third straight summer at the Five-Star Camp in Pennsylvania. Batesville's Siefert sized up the six-five-and-a-half Recker this way: "Luke Recker is by far the most gifted athlete in the state. He plays like he's seven feet."

Merrillville's Jamaal Davis received considerable media attention, too, but the headlines weren't always what he or his coach Jim East wanted. Some involved disagreements between them. Others pertained to Purdue's recruiting violations involving Davis. As a junior the big forward had averaged 19 points, 7.5 rebounds, and four blocked shots. East believed those numbers would have earned Davis far more headlines state-wide had he played outside "The Region" in northwestern Indiana. "We don't get the coverage. We get lost up here," said the coach. More people in Merrillville follow Chicago's professional teams, not Indianapolis's. Merrillville is on central time, not eastern. Pro star Glenn Robinson played in "The Region" and was Indiana's "Mr. Basketball" in 1991. But Robinson had gained wide recognition that season in part because he successfully led Gary Roosevelt through the tournament to the state championship. Before the 1996–97 season East applied to the Indiana Basketball Hall of Fame for a place in its four-team Christmas tournament. He wanted to "showcase" Davis and help Merrillville get its due. East was turned down. Hall of Fame officials decided a team other than Merrillville would attract a larger following of fans. "Merrillville deserved it and Jamaal deserved it," East said angrily. Both the seventeen-year-old star player and the fifty-six-year-old coach separately related tales of their sometimes strained relationship. But they shared certain feelings: that it was hard for teams and players in "The Region" to get attention throughout Indiana, that Merrillville High and its neighboring schools were in the Hoosier state but not wholly a part of it.

A Luke Recker story: On August 2, 1996, Alice Irene Girardot, ninety, lay dying in DeKalb Memorial Hospital in Auburn. It was between 11 A.M. and noon when Marti Recker, a nurse at Memorial, realized the end was near for the beloved area resident who had twenty-one grandchildren, forty-four great-grandchildren, and seven great-great-grandchildren. She loved Indiana University basketball, DeKalb basketball, and Marti's son, Luke. Oh how she loved Luke. Was it possible, she wondered, to meet him? "Of course," Marti said, and phoned him at home. Luke was there and came right over. The tall kid was taken aback when he reached the doorway of the hospital room, for suddenly he realized the gravity of the situation; the room was crowded with hospital attendants and family members. But the way was cleared and he was ushered to the woman's bedside. She took his hand. It was five minutes before noon. "I'm going to be with you," she said to him with a smile. "I'll be watching you." She died at 12:13.

A Jamaal Davis story: "I was born in East Chicago and I grew up in Gary. Gary is a survival place. If you can survive Gary, you can survive anyplace. You have pressure. You have different gangs up there. No matter where you live there's a gang set in that territory. Where I lived I was in the heart of Gary, in all of the killing, drug dealing, everything — I lived right there. The positive part I think of gangs is that they really looked out for me. Like if I'm in an area where something's going to go down, something's going to happen, it's 'Jamaal, go home.' There's a street out there called Fifth Avenue, I played basketball there, and they all watched to make sure nothing happened to me. They protect the people they think are worth protecting. Like they know I have a potential, a future, so they won't do anything to jeopardize what will happen. They encourage me to play. So that's why I didn't get in trouble with the gangs." Davis said that he had never been in a gang, but that only recently street life in Gary had deeply affected him. On November 12, 1996, the eve of his signing with Purdue, a friend had been slain in a drive-by shooting. The friend had been standing next to his flashy new car when he was hit by gunfire and died in the street. "His car was shot up," Davis said softly. "He was my friend." Davis dedicated his season to him.

Bob Knight wanted Recker for Indiana U. and getting him was easy.

Early in his sophomore season at DeKalb, Recker visited Bloomington for an Indiana-Iowa game and afterward was taken to the locker room and introduced to Knight. "Coach Knight pulled me off, took me back into a room, and told me, 'We want you.' I was kind of in awe because I was only a sophomore in high school and one of the greatest coaches ever was telling me 'We need you here to be part of our program.' That's when I really knew. I don't think there could be a more perfect place for me to play in the country, whether it be Duke, North Carolina, UCLA, or Kansas."

In the spring Recker went down to Bloomington again, with his mother, Marti, and his father, Clair. "We talked with Coach Knight for a long time. Some of the time we didn't even talk about basketball. But he told me what he expects of an Indiana basketball player, not only on the court but in the classroom, and how you're supposed to represent the program. Go to class. Get your grades. They do everything by the book there. And he asked me what I thought about that and I told him, 'I agree.' And he looked at my parents and my parents both said, 'We agree.'"

The Recker family had moved to Indiana from the northwestern Ohio town of Miller City when Luke was a fourth grader, and he soon thought of himself as "an Indiana kid." He'd wanted to play college ball in Indiana, where his family could watch him. Notre Dame didn't have a strong enough basketball tradition to interest him, even though someone from South Bend had phoned the Recker house expressing an interest in the boy after he had taken part in a summer camp there following eighth grade. Marti Recker recalled: "My husband thought somebody was playing a joke on him."

Two meetings with Knight were all Recker needed. From that time on he shrugged off suggestions to visit other schools before signing with Indiana. "I truly believed when I was a sophomore I wanted to go to Indiana, and I truly believe that now," he said. And so he signed on the first day of the signing period, November 13, 1996, a cold, snowy Wednesday at DeKalb. "Nothing could change my mind. Everybody said you can hold out and take your five official visits and go wherever you want and have people take you out. But that wasn't too attractive to me. Why would I waste other people's time and money?"

Jamaal Davis's college recruitment should have been as easy as Recker's. Davis wanted to go to Purdue as much as Recker wanted to go to Indiana. Glenn Robinson had gone there. "Purdue does a good job of recruiting 'The Region,'" East said. Davis also preferred Purdue because West Lafayette is only eighty miles south of Merrillville and his relatives could easily attend the games. "I like everything about Purdue," said Davis. But Purdue's pursuit of Davis took odd twists.

The Fort Wayne Journal-Gazette reported that Purdue had phoned Davis's father's home during a time when contact was not allowed. Purdue admitted it, with an explanation. The school reported itself to the NCAA for "inadvertent" minor recruiting violations: coaches had returned calls, not instigated them, and had never spoken with Davis. The calls, among other things, had to do with sales of candy; Davis's stepmother ran a candy business. Previously the candy business had led to trouble of another sort for Davis's stepmother.

Davis recalled, "My brother went to Horace Mann [High School in Gary]. [My stepmother,] my brother John, and my mother were there to put the candy in the concession stands. On the way out a couple guys stuck them up. Took my brother's coat off his back, his shoes off his feet. All my mom's rings, her wedding ring, purse, credit cards. My stepmother's. Their money." Belinda Brown, Davis's mother, said she lost $3,000 in company money from the business resource center she operated and that Davis's stepmother, Karen Davis, had just cashed her husband's paycheck and had $1,000 taken. Brown said: "They put a gun up to my son's head and asked for his coat and shoes. And you're standing there and watching this and you can't do anything for the child. He just came out of his stuff. It was December, it was cold. It was terrifying."

She had John move to Merrillville to live with his father and attend school there. And she decided to move out of Gary, too. The incident angered and dismayed Jamaal, but his mother expressed pride in his not getting involved by trying to retaliate against the perpetrators. The Davis brothers and their mother actually knew the youths who had held them up, she related. But she said she did not feel safe in identifying them. "We have no protection at all," she said.

Recker's only experience with inner-city life was a visit once to the Davises' former home in Gary, a small, tan brick house on a peaceful-looking street. Davis, Recker, and Cameron Stephens of Fort Wayne South Side, a Purdue recruit like Davis, stopped by there on their way to play in an all-star game in nearby East Chicago. Stephens is black, but Recker obviously was a stranger. Seeing him, black youths came up and "started talking California white talk . . . 'Oh, you have nice hair,'" Davis recalled. "He was worried. I said, 'They're just playing with you.'" To Recker's relief, they were.

But Recker's life was not as free of difficulty as it appeared. In the fall of 1996 he had to deal not with street crime but another widespread problem in American life, the broken home. In January 1995, Clair Recker received a job promotion that took him to Iowa, and now Clair and Marti's divorce was being finalized. The

Reckers had five children: Wendy, who was married, Annie, Luke, Maria, and Jackie. They were all basketball players, as their father had been at Bluffton College, in Bluffton, Ohio. If ever there seemed a model family, the Reckers were it. But Marti's eyes glazed as she said: "There isn't a mother who wouldn't like to have a son like Luke. He's been a big brother and a dad to his younger sisters."

Davis and Recker may have come from different backgrounds but they were alike in this respect: both loved the game and both had to cope with colossal expectations placed on them.

6

Crossroads of America

THE NARROW winding road along the southern border of the Hoosier National Forest is notable for its profound silence. It leads to Heltonville, and provides plenty of time to ponder how Damon Bailey emerged from such an obscure place to become the most revered player in Indiana high school basketball history.

His exploits had been known since Bob Knight discovered him in eighth grade. In his senior year of high school, 1990, he fulfilled all his promise in the state championship game. With Bedford North Lawrence down by six to the undefeated number one team in the state with two and a half minutes to play, Bailey scored the next 11 points to secure the triumph almost single-handedly, then ran into the crowd to embrace his parents, a former Heltonville High basketball player and a former Tunnelton High cheerleader.

Wendell's and Beverly's schools had merged to form Bedford North Lawrence, and the couple's own union had produced Damon.

He was pure Hooiser, modest and mannerly. Young boys modeled their lives on him, and because of him, men wished they could relive theirs. A couple named their son Damon and their daughter Bailey. A monument to Damon Bailey was built in Heltonville.

A simple green sign, HELTONVILLE, signaled arrival at the crossroads after miles of south-central Indiana hill and dale. It's a place of the mind more than anything, removed as it is even from the main road, U.S. 50, between Bedford and Seymour. Heltonville is a smattering of modest houses, small stores, and an orange-signed Union 76 gas station.

The monument sits atop a slope with a sidewalk leading up to it, next to the Heltonville Elementary School. The tribute is inscribed: "Damon Bailey: From your hometown fans in recognition of all you have achieved. With great pride and much love."

It's a sparkling limestone block carved in the shape of the state of Indiana with a star locating Heltonville. Bailey's portrait is chiseled at the top, and beneath it is a list of highlights from his high school and I.U. playing days: "All time leading scorer Indiana high school basketball. . . . Trester mental attitude award. . . . Gatorade national high school basketball player of the year. . . ." Bailey's anointing by Knight, a record-setting high school career with a storybook ending, and his often-expressed love for family combined to make him an icon usually referred to in Indiana by his first name only.

"Calling Damon Bailey the greatest player in Indiana history would be a dubious statement, but his hold on our collective imagination has been unparalleled," said Ron Newlin, former executive director of the Indiana Basketball Hall of Fame. "What he and that team accomplished ranks alongside Milan's victory in 1954 as a myth about what we want to believe is possible."

Off the white ribbons of interstate that slice Indiana like pieces of pie are other Heltonvilles. Many are named for a country or a foreign city; on the road from Jasper to Petersburg, in southwestern Indiana, you pass through, first, Ireland and, later, Algiers. Peru, up north between Logansport and Wabash, is a little bigger and has a pick of places to eat. There are towns named China, Holland, Morocco; Warsaw, Paris, Athens, Rome; towns with happy names — Birdseye and Santa Claus and Valentine and Popcorn and Bud. And in every one, kids shoot hoops year-round. Rick Mount shoots in a park in Lebanon.

"When basketball caught on in this state in the first two decades of the century, we were still a rural state, within some people's living memory of being a pioneer state," Newlin said. "Basketball appeals to the pioneer's belief in self-reliance. The sport is so well suited to solitary practice. How does one practice the basic skills of football or baseball by oneself? To be sure, there are fundamental basketball skills that are best developed in competition. But the classic image of the Indiana basketball star is a figure such as Rick Mount or Steve Alford, refining his skills with endless hours of repetition, alone in a gym while others are out swimming or eating pizza. We want our heroes to be *made*, not born — preferably *self-made*."

The game is still played in barns. It's played on driveways, at playgrounds, in alleys. Indiana's beacon remains the outdoor basketball hoop, even if these days a hoop next to a home often shares the horizon with a satellite dish.

Indiana kids still dream of making the high school team more than anything else. It makes them feel more exalted — even more so than driving around Monument Circle in Indianapolis on a Saturday night with a car full of friends and the radio blaring. Not making the high school basketball team can be a time worse than a kid has ever known and one he'll never forget. The 1996–97 season was almost at hand when Batesville's Melvin Siefert said: "Every year about this time I get this feeling, right here in my gut. I have twenty-seven boys who want to play and I have to make a determination. I talk to each of them individually. I tell them, not everybody can be a basketball player, and everybody has to find a niche someplace. I try to help them. If I have to have six team managers because they still want to be part of it, I'll have six team managers. But telling a kid you don't think you can use him is like telling a kid he just lost a member of his family. That's basketball in Indiana."

In Indiana people know that Tom Coverdale is the Noblesville guard, and that lean Kueth Duany is Bloomington North's big man — even in an era when so many sports and other diversions would suggest a diminishing interest in high school ball. Even if people had never seen certain players because they played in different parts of the state — "Is Menser really as good as they say?" asked a man from upstate — they knew who was playing and talked about them as if they had firsthand knowledge. Of course that's how legend is spread.

"The thing you have here is that when you go to a game there really are a hell of a lot of knowledgeable people there," said Bob Knight. "They've been following basketball for years. They've seen great basketball, they've enjoyed it, they know what it is."

Towns are associated with players. "Lebanon: Home of Rick Mount." Plymouth is Scott Skiles's town; Skiles led the Pilgrims to the 1982 championship in two overtimes against Gary Roosevelt. "He could go back and be mayor if he wanted," said Mike Springer, an assistant coach with the Logansport Berries. In Indianapolis, the sprawling red brick buildings of Crispus Attucks, now a junior high school, bring to mind one player: Oscar Robertson.

It's almost impossible to travel through the southwestern part of Indiana without thinking of the most famous person to grow up there. Larry Bird is merely the most famous basketball player from the area. Driving through wooded hills across the bottom of the state you think of a United States president. You're in the land of Lincoln's boyhood. Parts of the area remain remote enough to conjure thoughts of two centuries ago, when the Lincoln family arrived from Kentucky. In Carl Sandburg's history of Lincoln, seven-year-old Abe joined his father, Tom, in hacking a path with axes through forest and underbrush as Abe's mother, Nancy, and older sister, Sarah, followed. They stopped and stayed at a clearing near Little Pigeon Creek, sixteen miles north of the Ohio River. It was December 1816. As Sandburg related from Lincoln's own account, the boy sometimes experienced a frightful time in the wild place where "the panther's scream filled night with fear" and "bears preyed on the swine." Lincoln estimated that each square mile contained one person.

Where Lincoln lived for fourteen years, the hundred-plus acres seemed still to be as Lincoln described them: with every step you could touch a tree. The place is near a crossroads called Lincoln City. A doe leaped out of the woods and bounded across a knoll near the fenced graveyard where Nancy Hanks Lincoln is buried.

French Lick, where Bird was a boy, is just a short drive north of Lincoln's home. French Lick once was a resort to which vacationers flocked, often by rail. But Bird plaintively recalled a coming-of-age struggle in a land that could be discouragingly unyielding: "Life was the same for all my friends at home. You just didn't know it until you got out, then you said, God, that's not the way it's supposed to be. We didn't have money. We didn't go hungry. We had plenty to eat. But we just never had a family car, a family vacation. There wasn't a lot of industry down there. When you was laid off, you was laid off. You didn't know when you'd go back to work."

A man who was raised nearby at about the same time as Bird related that his father, a doctor, made house calls to deliver babies, but that money was so tight, his fee of twenty-five dollars often went uncollected. As those children grew up, he would know the ones who weren't "paid for." As young Lincoln did, young Bird experienced the death of a parent — in his case the suicide of a father who knew divorce and enduring poverty.

In October 1996, Larry Bird's mother, Georgia, died and was buried in the Crystal Community Cemetery, midway between French Lick and Haysville, so small it was easy to miss even with directions. "You know why they call it Crystal, don't you?" said Cyril Birge, of Jasper. "Because you can see clear through it."

It was slow going on shoulderless Route 56 behind a truck carrying logs. The cemetery spread across a hillside above a barn and a shed. Halfway up a gravel path was Georgia Bird's headstone already in place. A rectangle of earth had been newly turned next to where her estranged husband lay buried. Georgia M., 1930–1996. Claude J. Jr., 1926–1975. Together again.

There, on a peaceful hill with a vista of unsullied land, the simplicity of Bird's early life could be felt. The only sound was the hum of cars and trucks below as they swept through Crystal.

One evening in November in Princeton, Indiana, not far from French Lick, well-regarded Vincennes Lincoln and three other teams took part in a jamboree, a kind of preseason dress rehearsal popular in Indiana basketball. A man behind the counter at CarQuest Auto Parts in Princeton pointed toward the middle school, where the jamboree would be held. Princeton Community High plays at the middle school, which once was the high school, because the old gym is bigger than the one at the new school. "About the only thing it has going for it is the gym," the CarQuest man said.

Tony Cloyd, a radio play-by-play broadcaster from Vincennes, plugged in and set up to broadcast what in effect would be only half a game. In a jamboree four or more teams gather with each team allowed to play two quarters, either against two different teams or the same team. Vincennes Lincoln would play its two eight-minute quarters against Mt. Vernon; Princeton would play Boonville. The Vincennes announcer unfurled a WFML-FM station banner: "The Alices Fly on the Eagle, 96.7."

The name Alices came from the title character in a book called *Alice of Old Vincennes*, about a woman who aided a Revolutionary War soldier. It's an eye-catcher when the boys from Vincennes take the floor for warm-ups in their silky green sweatsuits with "Alices" across the front.

Gene Miiller, whose name looks like a typo, was beginning his sixteenth season as coach. A tall man with glasses and close-cropped black hair, he took the 1984 Alices to the state championship game, only to lose to Warsaw. "We got there with five kids who just loved to play basketball every day," said Miiller. "No superstars. Nobody who made an all-star team. It's what Indiana basketball is all about. I don't know why you'd change the greatest tournament in the world."

"We still watch the tape of the last game quite often," said Miiller's wife, Debbie, sitting behind the team bench. "Brings tears every time."

Heather, the youngest of their three daughters, was among the cheerleaders — the Alices were going into this glorified scrimmage with all their cheerleaders if not all their players. The starting point guard was still playing football. So Miiller decided to see how four forwards and a center could handle the ball.

The half game began, and seconds later: "On his shoulder, ref!" It was a woman in the Alices' cheering section. She continued to work the officials even though it was hardly more than a practice. The officials looked like twins. Both were short, with blond hair parted on the right. They weren't twins but they were brothers. The Peach boys, Phil and Paul. They pretended not to hear.

Mt. Vernon took a 10–3 lead, 14–11 at the period. Calmly, Miiller knelt before his players seated on the bench, dispensing strategy in a deep, succinct voice. He concluded with a confident appraisal of how they could reach the basket: "You can go inside and score anytime you want." A couple of the Alices looked up as if they'd just been handed English translations of the *Odyssey*.

Drive they did. It was that easy. They went on a 17—4 run and won, 32—22.

"I want to play another half," said the woman who'd been shouting.

"It's just the appetizer," a man reassured her.

Miiller and his players watched half of the half between Princeton and Boonville before getting back on their bus. As he turned to leave, Miiller said: "This is the championship that everyone will be shooting for. It'll be a big one. These'll be the last true champions."

7

A Beginning

ANDERSON High School is an old red-brick building with an even larger building looming up behind it like a huge tortoise shell. The larger building is the basketball gym. An Indian mosaic on the outside wall to the right of Gate 1 dominates the view from the parking lot. More than 80,000 pieces of colored tile were used to put together the Indian chief, a state landmark. Anderson's nickname is the Indians, of course, and nowhere in a state whose name means the "land of the Indians" is Indian tradition taken more seriously than at Anderson High. There is only one gym like Anderson High's. It's called the Wigwam.

On November 29, 1996, the opening of the home season, everything about the place is old and used but glistening clean and neat. The smell of fresh popcorn permeates the atmosphere, and the feeling you get walking in is that of coming home, of taking your coat off, relaxing.

The Wigwam opened in November 1961, replacing a smaller Wigwam that burned down. It's intimate in that everything is close: the narrow corridors, the concession stands, the pinched entryways to courtside, even the majority of vantage points over-looking the gleaming hardwood floor. Yet standing next to that floor, looking around, you feel the massiveness of an almost 9,000-seat building. In Indiana high school basketball, the Wig-wam is the Louvre.

"We have the second largest high school gym in the world but the best atmosphere," said Ron Hecklinski. "There's no place in the world I'd rather coach than in the Wigwam. Wait'll you see the pregame festivities."

Hecklinski's office looks like the oldest part of the building. A brown sofa sags close to the ground. Trophies and team photos fill every cranny. Aphorisms cover the walls of the room and the corridor outside. A frayed Converse poster of Larry Bird diving for a loose ball bears the caption: "It makes me sick when I see a guy just watching it go out of bounds." Another maxim is posted near it: "I did the best I could . . . and I'll keep right on doing it up to the end. . . ." Words of Abraham Lincoln.

Hecklinski, seated at his desk, took out a blank lineup card and a pen, and turned to the dean of students, Pete Danforth, who was sitting on the sofa. "You can fill it out tonight. You tell me the names," the coach said. Hecklinski was so happy to be there that occasionally he would forget about his physical condition. His stomach still was so swollen from surgery that he couldn't get his trousers on and had to coach wearing a red sweatsuit. Red and green are Anderson's colors. Everything in the Wigwam was decorated in red and green, and in the pep section most of the men and women wore the colors. Many were senior citizens who'd graduated from Anderson and held season tickets ever since.

As Hecklinski hunched over his lineup card the dean ticked off one name and then a second and the coach filled them in. But the third name came as a surprise to Hecklinski. He shot Danforth a look and wrote the name he wanted. He finished the lineup card himself over the dean's feigned protest. "I thought we were on the same page," Hecklinski said to him.

A small man walked right into the room. "I'm glad you're back," he addressed Hecklinski. He was a fan of the Indians. "Keep on doing what you're doing and you'll have a winning team," he told the coach, and presented him with two tickets to a dinner theater. Hecklinski thanked him profusely, but couldn't remember his name. The man then leaned forward over Hecklinski's desk and gave final instructions: "Stay on 'em. Kick 'em in the butt a little bit. We want a winning season."

That's how it is in Indiana. Have your liver out, but remember: win.

For the pregame show, the place was more than half full. The eighty boys and girls of the band struck up from the stage behind one basket, the pep-section rooters got to their feet clapping, everyone stood, nine student drummers came quick-stepping onto the court followed by twelve flag bearers and sixteen cheerleaders. The lights were shut off and a spotlight shone on the court, leaving the edges of the arena bathed in the glow of orange and red from the letters and numbers on the four-sided electric scoreboard above center court. A color guard of five marched on and the public address announcer, seated at the scorer's table, took command in a blaring voice:

"The flag is the symbol of our national unity.

"It tells us of the struggle for independence, of unity preserved, of liberty, and of the sacrifices of brave men and women.

"It means America first. It means an undivided allegiance.

"It means that we cannot be saved by the courage of our ancestors.

"That to each generation comes its patriotic duty and that upon

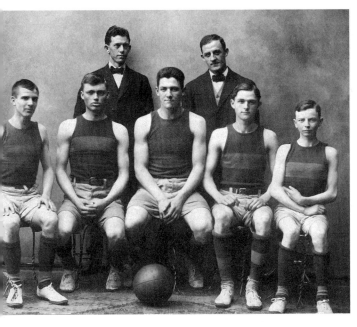

The Crawfordsville Athenians of 1906. Basketball began in Indiana in Crawfordsville, known as the "Athens of Indiana."

Indiana Basketball Hall of Fame

John Wooden, who coached UCLA to ten NCAA championships, played on three straight Indiana high school state final teams with Martinsville (1926–28). Martinsville won the state title in 1927. He was a three-time All-American at Purdue.

Indiana Basketball Hall of Fame

Hammond, Indiana, welcomes home the 1940 state champion, Hammond Tech.

Indiana Basketball Hall of Fame

The State Fairgrounds Coliseum in Indianapolis was the site of the state championship games from 1943 to 1945.

Indiana Basketball Hall of Fame

From 1928 to 1935, Butler University coach Tony Hinkle (right) and *Indianapolis News* sportwriter Bill Fox visited each "sweet sixteen" team in a Stutz Bearcat. Hinkle was looking for recruits and Fox was looking for stories to write.

The Wingate gym became home for Wingate's "gymless wonders" after they won state titles in 1913 and 1914.

James Dean, Fairmount guard in the late 1940s, before he left Indiana for Hollywood.
Collection of David Loehr/The James Dean Gallery, Fairmount, Indiana

Carl Erskine (left), one of the Brooklyn Dodgers' "Boys of Summer," and Johnny Wilson, former Harlem Globetrotter, were basketball teammates at Anderson High in the 1940s.

Damon Bailey, with his mother, Beverly, and sister, Courtney, after leading Bedford North Lawrence to the 1990 championship before a record high school crowd of 41,046.
Mark Wick, courtesy of the Indiana High School Athletic Association.

Larry Bird, Springs Valley High, 1974, was the self-proclaimed "Hick from French Lick."
Indiana Basketball Hall of Fame

DeKalb's Luke Recker dunking.

Mark Murdock, *Auburn Evening Star*

Recker signs to attend Indiana University. With him are his mother, Marti, his coach, Cliff Hawkins, and his sisters, Annie, Jackie, and Maria.

Mark Murdock, *Auburn Evening Star*

our willingness to sacrifice and endure rests the hope of this nation.

"I am proud of our past!

"I am proud of our heritage!

"I am proud to be . . . an American!"

The band played "The Star Spangled Banner." Then a student carried out the biggest drum of all onto the court. An "Indian maiden" and an "Indian" ran out from different corners. To the drumbeat they performed an Indian dance in the spotlight at midcourt. It's said at Anderson High that the "maiden" and the "Indian" are the two most coveted positions students can hold, with the exception of a spot on the basketball roster.

The lights came up, everyone marched off, and two men pushing wide mops briskly cleaned the court. Mopping basketball floors in Indiana is a pregame ritual that's been raised almost to an art, as men bend to get every speck of dust. The PA announcer exuberantly proclaimed, "Welcome, sports fans, to the Wigwam." Then the overhead lights were lowered, the Anderson players introduced in a spotlight. Hecklinski received sustained applause, which he acknowledged with his right hand. His left arm still hung limply.

The ten-minute ceremony was repeated before every home game, as it has been since 1945, in the old Wigwam. The first "Indian maiden" only sang. But a late-forties "maiden" had a ballroom dance partner and the two performed at a pep rally. The basketball coach asked them to dance before a ball game, and during the 1949–50 season the "maiden" and the "Indian" pregame routine began its long-playing run in Anderson. Much of the dance itself and the Indian attire are authentic, according to Wendell Hilligoss, retired chairman of the school's business department, who for twenty-five years was the sponsor of the mascot and "maiden." He said that the Indian headdress was made in a western tribal style and the breastplate derived from animal bones, the loin cloth beaded in Indian design, the leggings sewn in traditional

Indian style. In 1981 the clothing was stolen from the mascot's car but later recovered, somewhat damaged. A person from Indianapolis who was part Native American helped restore it.

"We practice a ceremony of respect," said Doug Vermillion, the public address announcer and chairman of the social studies department. Throughout Indiana the ceremony was well-known and liked — though in some parts of the country it would hardly be considered "politically correct." Vermillion, who is part Indian, insisted that Native Americans would approve.

Vermillion said that the issue at Anderson High was not the pregame ceremony but the scheduled closing of the building at the end of the school year. The city's school board had deemed it more practical financially to consolidate three high schools into two. Only recently had the school colors and nickname and pageantry, and the Wigwam itself, been saved from extinction, even though Anderson's students would be reassigned to either Madison Heights or Highland. Madison Heights, on the south side of the city, would become known as Anderson High — in part a concession to the large number of Anderson High grads angered by their school's closing. Madison Heights's nickname of Pirates and its colors, red and black, would disappear — to the anger and disappointment of their partisans. The Indians would commute to play their home games in the Wigwam.

Change confronted people in Anderson. The end of the single basketball tournament was dramatic enough, but closing Anderson High was entirely unsettling. Part of the building — spacious, three stories — dated from 1910. Anderson High had graduated more than 30,000 students. The place on Lincoln Street between Thirteenth and Fourteenth had remained a fixture even as life in Anderson, once an automaking hub, had changed. AHS, as it was abbreviated, had been a constant in a world of turmoil.

"This is the last public connection we have to Anderson's past that's still being used for its originally intended purpose," Vermillion said.

"It's built like a bomb shelter," said Hilligoss. "It's double-bricked with concrete blocks behind that. They don't build things like that anymore."

One of the three high school basketball coaches in town would lose his job. Each officially would be out of work at the end of the year and have to reapply. A committee of eleven school officials would select the two coaches for 1997–98 after interviewing the applicants. Nothing was guaranteed for Hecklinski, despite his comeback-in-progress, despite his record. "Before the transplant we would have been worried about the job," said Pam Hecklinski. "Now, whatever happens, it'll be all right."

Pam watched the games in the Wigwam from the front row at the baseline near the Anderson bench, and these days she watched her husband closely because he had been working too hard despite his promises to her. He had been trying to improve his team's play — correcting, urging, as weak as he was — because Anderson had been surprised in its opener on the road, at North Central. That was the first time anyone around had seen the "move-in" Huggy Dye play, and he'd made the difference in a high-speed 82–78 game.

The defeat dropped Anderson from its lofty preseason rankings in the state's two weekly high school polls, which are followed religiously by fans. Anderson fell from second to eighth in the coaches' poll and from third to ninth in the media poll conducted by the Associated Press. Anderson had won its next game, and now Hecklinski had two home games to be sure he had the team righted. This night the opponent was Daleville, which had only 200 students compared with Anderson's 1,026. Two radio stations carried the Anderson games; the play-by-play men sat two rows behind Hecklinski's wife. Assistants Terry Turner and John Wilson flanked Hecklinski on the bench.

Eric Bush hoped to be the new Johnny Wilson by leading Anderson to its first state title since 1946, and many in the crowd, leaning forward in anticipation, came to measure Bush's progress.

Daleville never could catch up to him. Bush got the team's fast break working and led a 7–0 run that put Anderson ahead 23–14 at the end of the first quarter. An Anderson aide slipped a stool under Hecklinski so he could talk with his players seated in front of him on the bench. "He needs to sit," said Pam. "He can't bend over because of his stomach."

By the second period, Hecklinski's daughter, Stephanie, and a playmate, both dressed in Anderson red and green, colored in their books on the floor. Anderson won, 86–54. As the players left the court each touched a glass case that held part of the original Wigwam floor.

Alexandria High, four nights later, proved more of a challenge than had Daleville. A school of about 575 students, Alexandria had a history of success against larger schools because of an outstanding coach, a wiry man named Garth Cone. Cone loved single-class basketball because he loved to spring upsets of larger schools. And he did so with regularity. Now, even with several good players having graduated, Cone conceded nothing to Anderson. The players with "Alex" on their shirts fell behind by fifteen points. They were shorter and forced into a zone defense. But Cone kept calling plays until "Alex" trailed by only 47–44 with 2:22 left. It was then that Bush broke free, was fouled, and made two free throws. Anderson survived, 59–50. But Anderson did not look like a championship team.

Anderson had a history, before Hecklinski's arrival, of falling short. The Indians lost four state championship games from 1979 through 1986 under Hecklinski's predecessor, Norm Held. It took one only a couple of visits to Anderson before this sarcasm surfaced: "Did you know they named a street in Anderson after Norm Held? Second Street."

Ben Davis coach Steve Witty said that Anderson teams "have a tendency to turn it on and off." And that's how Anderson played against Alexandria, in spurts, as if wanting to do no more than necessary. Hecklinski was furious. He was worried about the conference opener in three days at rival Marion. Anderson and Marion belong to the highly competitive North Central Conference, one of the country's oldest leagues. It is a collection of small-city teams: Anderson, Marion, Muncie Central, Richmond, New Castle, Kokomo, Lafayette Jefferson, and Logansport. The conference bills itself as the "Conference of Champions"; Muncie Central has won more state championships than any Indiana school, eight; and Marion had won five, including three in a row in the eighties. It was difficult winning on the road in the league, which Hecklinski well knew. Anderson hadn't won at Marion in eighteen years.

He stormed through the doorway to the players' locker room faster than anyone had seen him move since his surgery. The room was small, cozy, with thick, wall-to-wall red carpeting and, for more carefree times, a boom box to blast rap music. For now the only sound was Hecklinski's voice as the players sat on stools in front of their lockers. As loud as he spoke, however, he couldn't be heard outside the room because of the building's thick walls and heavy doors.

"Let me tell you something," he said angrily. He was standing in the middle of the room and, new liver or not, he was standing straight. "Let me tell you something right now. You are all headed in the wrong direction. Offensively you've got no clue about moving the ball. You think that offensive basketball means you dribble. You get a fifteen-point lead and you go one-on-one. You want to have a team with seven guys who average twenty points. You're out there trying to score 140 points instead of moving and getting each other open. You realize what a good team would have done to you tonight? Marion will beat you if you play like that.

"I heard 'em talking in the stands. 'C'mon, coach, make 'em run some offense.' They're right. We've got to move the ball. We've got to take care of the ball. How many times do I have to tell you? Don't you get tired of hearing me tell you the same thing? I don't like this performance at all. I don't like it one bit. You were walking around out there. Oh, shit, we're cool. Not till the last two minutes did you get revved up.

"It's the mentality of the whole team that bothers me. I've got to get mine, instead of moving the ball. You guys make the game hard. Make the game simple. Alexandria makes the game simple. Make the simple pass. We all know you can play. You don't have to impress anybody.

"We've got a lot of work to do, boys. We've got a lot of work to do. Unless you put in that work you won't have the great team you think you are. Defensively you played hard and that's what kept you in the game. But start exploiting people offensively. We're going to go one and a half hard hours tomorrow, one and a half hard hours Thursday. There's been a lot of great Marion games. It's going to be a hard-ass game. Tomorrow — no dribbling allowed in practice. No dribbling. Get home. Get some rest. Get on the books. Let's get to work tomorrow.

"One, two, three . . ."

The players stacked hands and shouted, "Team together."

Another coach had words for his team.

"Allow nothing in the fifteen-foot area. All shots are contested, and then block out. One shot if at all. We want flat-out domination. If the ball gets down in the paint, dive down there and get it. You're not playing Garrett. You are playing against your own potential to be the greatest team in the state of Indiana — that's what you're playing against tonight. Be aggressive. Be enthusiastic. Dive on the floor for the balls. Play with your hearts. Go out and get the job done."

The DeKalb Barons yelled as one and jumped up from chairs that had been perfectly aligned in front of a blackboard Cliff Hawkins had used before his summary call to perfection. The players bunched up at the doorway as they heard "The Star Spangled Banner"; some were breathing hard. When the anthem ended they rushed out single-file, bending to the right as they passed a set of bleachers, and ran confidently onto their home court. Applause and cheers from a standing-room crowd of 3,000 washed over them, and from the far side of the court the DeKalb pep band offered a glorious full-blast greeting from its puffed-cheeked, red-faced brass blowers.

This, Friday, December 6, was just another night in Indiana. The Garrett Railroaders were not expected to offer much competition. But now Luke Recker was a senior, the Barons were coming off a 24–2 season, and both the media and coaches' polls had ranked DeKalb tenth in the state preseason. During a recent practice Hawkins's starters denied his second team a basket seventeen straight possessions — that kind of defense pleased him. "We want to set the tone defensively," he said, "then get flying up the floor." The team played tough defense — and it had speed. Most of all, it had Recker.

Watching the kid known as "Luke Skywalker" gave people in DeKalb County, and especially Hawkins, visions of a state championship. Hawkins might never get closer. This was his fourth stop as a varsity coach, having progressed from tiny Caston High, in Fulton in north-central Indiana, to Tri-Central in Sharpsville, north of Indianapolis, to Greenfield. Along the way Hawkins had acquired a reputation for such attention to detail that he usually slept only four hours a night. He liked to cover locker-room walls with homemade motivational posters ("For us excellence is an aspiration, an attitude, a pursuit, a way of life; excellence is all of us working together aspiring to the fullness of our potential"). He affixed handwritten messages to his assistant coaches' lockers ("Coach: What will you do today to help us become the champion?"). He was even known for gimmickry. Even gimmickry that didn't work.

The jockstrap story: "Tri-Central had only two winning seasons in fifteen years, and so we go to Clinton Prairie on the road and we have a chance to win a conference championship," Hawkins said. "But we were playing just a superb Clinton Prairie team. Prior to that I had asked everybody to bring in a jockstrap that week. I said, 'The reason I want you to bring in jockstraps is that some of the underprivileged kids in our middle school program need jockstraps.' But that wasn't the truth. In the meantime, I had my manager get me a metal bucket and some lighter fluid and some matches. My theme for the game was 'Burn the Gophers.'

"So I bring 'em into the locker room, I make everybody sit in the shower room, and I say, 'We're going to burn away this terrible tradition of losing.' And I took my match and threw it into that bucket and the jockstraps just burned. Okay, so we're all rah-rah-rah. Well, we're still not good enough to beat those people that year. The bottom line is it's halftime, I'm walking across the floor and the principal of Clinton Prairie stops me and he goes, 'Cliff, there's been a fire in your locker room.' I said, 'Charlie, I know, I set it.' I explain to him what I was trying to do and it was okay, he understood. Well, what happens is, the story gets out that I'm upset about the loss and I tried to burn the building down."

Hawkins arrived at DeKalb with ambition but with no knowledge of a rising eighth grader named Recker. "I just wanted to get a step closer to winning the state championship by coming here," he said.

Now he was poised to take that step. In 1995–96 Recker had led DeKalb to twenty straight victories while averaging 21.7 points and 6.1 assists. DeKalb won the Northeast Hoosier Conference, then three games in the tournament sectional, then the first game of its regional. But DeKalb lost the night game of the regional to Fort Wayne's Bishop Dwenger, which had handed DeKalb its only other loss of the season. The name Dwenger never had completely stopped ricocheting in Hawkins's mind.

During the summer he'd called a "coaching retreat" for his staff in an effort to eliminate future Dwengers. They'd repaired to the Holiday Inn in Angola, near the Michigan-Ohio border, and there studied upcoming opponents and possible tournament scenarios as if seeking the secrets of Stonehenge.

Hawkins awakened at 4:30 every morning to begin watching film, devising strategy, sifting mounds of information that might make the difference in a close game, thinking of new ways to inspire his team. "I wasn't a good player, I never played on a great high school team," he said. "Maybe that's why I've always wanted to do this as well as I could." Hawkins set an agenda on his "coaching retreat" that called for his assistants to explore ways to improve their coaching. "Just because Luke Recker's a great player, we don't quit coaching," he told them. "We've got to take him to the next level." He told his coaches, "You can't depend on me to supply all the basketball knowledge. We may be coaching a potential NBA player. What do we need to do with this kid?"

As part of his effort to get his star player prepared in every way for his senior season, Hawkins asked Recker if he was coping well enough with his father's absence. It was the summer of 1996, and they were driving in Indianapolis at the time of the Nike camp. "It's tough," Luke told Hawkins. "But the people I worry about most are my mother and my sisters."

"What about you?" Hawkins asked again, driving along.

"It bothers me," Luke replied, "but it's not going to keep me from accomplishing what I want to accomplish."

Hawkins brought the subject up another time when the two were alone in the DeKalb gym. Luke was shooting baskets and Hawkins was catching the shots and flipping the ball back. Hawkins liked to double-check everything.

"I said, 'How bad is this going to bother you?'" Hawkins recalled. "And he said, 'I've already had to adjust to my father not being here.' I was really concerned about him. This is the essence of coaching, building that relationship with kids and letting them know you care."

Recker knew exactly how Hawkins felt about him. Hawkins had called it an "honor" to be his coach.

Recker could read of Bob Knight's lavish praise of him in the Auburn paper. After Recker had signed his letter of intent, Knight told Mark Murdock of the Evening Star: "I saw him when he was a sophomore and he was six four. He was a great athlete with great basketball skills, and we thought he was the exact prototype of the kind of player that had been so good for us over the years. We've seen him play over the last year and a half or two years, and he's gotten better and better. He's also gotten bigger and stronger. He's probably the first since [Calbert] Cheaney who's as good at doing all the different things." Cheaney became the Big Ten's all-time leading scorer and was the college player of the year as a senior in 1993.

"From the first time I met him, I've been very impressed," Knight said of Recker. "He's one of those kids that you say, 'We've just got to have him.'"

Knight was more restrained, but not by much, during a conversation about Recker in Bloomington. "We got a film and looked at him and then brought him down, and I just really liked the looks of the kid. I remember we were talking after — here's a kid, just a sophomore, I think he was only fifteen years old. But he was six four, was wiry, and just really looked like he could play. In fact that's what we need more than anything right now, a kid who is six five or six six who can play."

"What is Recker now?" Knight asked an assistant.

"Hundred and ninety, six five and a half."

"He couldn't have weighed one seventy when we first saw him."

Recker would get stronger, heavier, maybe a shade taller. But Knight revised his earlier comparison of Recker and Cheaney. "He's more like [Randy] Wittman," the coach said. Wittman helped Indiana to the 1981 national championship and averaged 19 points his senior year in 1983. He then played nine unspectacular seasons in the NBA. But Knight said enthusiastically: "Wittman's one of the two or three best players we've had here. I don't think I had seen anybody I thought was close to being as good as Wittman was until this kid came along. This kid's got a chance to be a really good player. Cheaney was really a scorer. Wittman was just a great all-around player.''

From the start of play against Garrett it was clear why Knight felt as he did about Recker. DeKalb's number 24 sprang out on the Garrett ball handler and, with a long-armed swat, blocked his attempt at a three-pointer. The ball bounced high near midcourt and, running easily ahead of everyone, Recker gathered it in, took three immense strides, twisted in the air, and with his back to the basket remained elevated while eschewing a rim-rattling reverse dunk. Instead, he held the ball over his head and deposited it into the net as gently as a grocery-store checker placing ripe fruit into a shopping bag.

Recker's ability to leap and glide on air was part of his renown. When he moved with the ball, people edged forward on their seats wondering whether he would score on a slam dunk or a reverse dunk or a pull-up jump shot or some kind of shot they hadn't seen. Possibly he would use his left hand to drop the ball effortlessly into the net after rising above it. He was going to score, for sure; it was just a question of which grace note he would strike.

His mother had a collection of scrapbooks and newspaper accounts about him, enough to fill a shopping bag. All the write-ups were glowing.

Could this avalanche of accolades affect him? Even playing in a small town didn't alleviate the pressure put on some Indiana high school players. Whereas the Indianapolis Star's thorough high school coverage has to be diffused because of the number of teams in its circulation area, a town paper and area television stations tend to home in on the home school team. Recker also attracted media from well beyond the DeKalb High area. In his senior year that attention would only increase, with perhaps still more pressure. It could well be, however, that this special player on whom the coach counted so heavily, the young man who, according to his mother, had taken over the role of "man of the house," possessed the disposition and character to shoulder all responsibilities. His senior season would be his greatest chance for high school glory, but it could also be a time of heroic failure. Even an outcome somewhere in between would be much publicized and pressurized.

Michael Lewis's mother, Cathy, said that her son experienced more pressure during his senior year at Jasper High than during his freshman year at Indiana, even under the disciplinarian Knight. "At Jasper he was counted on every game to score thirty points," she said. "That's a lot of pressure. At Indiana Michael is surrounded by great players and he's not counted on the way he was in high school."

In the third quarter of the lopsided game against Garrett, Recker glided above the floor à la Michael Jordan before stuffing the ball into the basket at the end of a fast break. During a fourth-period curtain call he swiped an inbounds pass and stuffed the ball again. With four minutes to play and DeKalb romping 75–35 Hawkins sat him down. He had 27 points. Immediately people got up, coats in hand, and made their way down the steps to the exits. The show was over.

Later Hawkins told a reporter that Recker's performance was "incredible." The coach then phoned in to a popular radio program, "Network Indiana: Indiana Sports Talk," which featured live interviews with high school coaches, at least those whose teams had won. When host Bob Lovell's voice faded on your car radio it would come in clear on another station from another town. On game nights in Indiana the talk was about Indiana's game.

Because of the seven-second broadcast delay Hawkins stretched the phone cord from his office desk into the adjoining bathroom and closed the door so his assistants could listen on radio. Hawkins had to wait in there because Steve Witty was on the air. Ben Davis had won its opener, but Witty said, "I'd like to see 'em play with a

lot more intensity than we had tonight. We did not execute well."
Witty's prognosis for the game the next night at Pike, another
Indianapolis power, sounded overly pessimistic: "If we play
against them like we played tonight, we'll get beat by thirty." His
prognosis would be proven accurate enough; Ben Davis would
lose by four.

On "Network Indiana" Lovell wanted Hawkins to tell him everything Recker had done, and Hawkins gave those statistics —
the 27 points, eight rebounds, five assists, three steals, eight deflections. That was on top of the 40 points Recker scored in De-
Kalb's opening victory against Northrop. The caliber of DeKalb's
first two opponents and the whole stretch of season that Recker
still had to carry this team were all but forgotten as radio voices
in the night spread his fame.

Numerous high-scoring guards in bygone Indiana seasons had
been asked to lead role-playing teammates to a state championship.
Rick Mount, Kyle Macy, and Steve Alford were among the most
famous. Only Damon Bailey had succeeded. In Indiana not only
was Bailey known by his first name only but he was sometimes
even referred to as "the baby boy Jesus."

Recker was only two games into his senior season, but he had
no way to stop people from dreaming that he would be another
Damon. After the Garrett game Hawkins and his assistants joined
their wives and some friends at the home of their athletic director,
Dick McKean. At about 11:20 McKean worked the remote so that
they got to see the sports on all the Fort Wayne channels. One led
the high school coverage with Recker's block and reverse lay-in,
which drew hearty approval from the living-room crowd.

How Anderson did at Marion went unreported. But one of
Hawkins's assistants, Rod Cone, had heard the score driving over
from the gym. Cone was the son of Alexandria coach Garth Cone,
part of an Indiana tradition of coaches raising sons who became
coaches.

"Anderson beat Marion 76–67," Rod Cone said. Bush had

scored 26 points in the first half. Hecklinski's tirade after Anderson's last game hadn't hurt.

Milan was Batesville's sixth game of the season, but people in Batesville still were talking about the finish of the opening game. Batesville's opponent that night had been a familiar one, South Dearborn, the team Michael Menser dribbled through and defeated the previous season with his shot that fell in after the buzzer. It didn't seem possible that Batesville could cut victory any closer, but then there seemed no limit to the improbable when Batesville and South Dearborn got together.

This time, as the final seconds ticked away, the South Dearborn Knights again had the lead, by a point — and this time they had the ball. In the last second Batesville fouled, a roar went up from the South Dearborn home crowd, and, thinking that time had expired, South Dearborn's coach and others charged onto the court to celebrate. The official informed the South Dearborn coach that one second remained and that he was charged with a technical. South Dearborn missed the front end of its one-and-one free-throw opportunity. Then Michael Menser — who else? — sank the two shots awarded on the technical and, like that, Batesville had rung up yet another victory over South Dearborn by the demoralizing margin of one point.

Menser also took care of Batesville's fourth victory to preserve its state ranking — fourteenth by the coaches and fifteenth by the media. He scored 48 points at nearby Greensburg, site of the sectional that Batesville would be playing in, come tournament time. One of Menser's plays added to his legend. He was driving to the basket for a layup when a Greensburg player successfully blocked his path. Menser, already airborne, looked to pass off. But his teammate alongside also was covered. On the way down Menser scooped the ball underhanded up and over his defender and into the basket.

Jenny Menser, Michael's mother, said that Batesville's rooters were able to keep their thriller victories and Michael's heroics in perspective because of Batesville's last-second loss in the previous season's regional at New Castle. A small woman, Jenny Menser got into the games in a big way. The second-grade teacher cheered so loudly that her quiet husband, Jim, usually sat many rows apart from her.

Jenny, everyone knew, had something to do with developing Michael's shooting touch. "Being a teacher she had the keys to the gyms and she used to unlock them and sit in there and grade papers while the kid shot around," said Milan coach Randy Combs. Actually it was a little more than that.

"Michael would have the ball at center court and I would pretend to be the announcer," said Jenny Menser. "The score would always be 69–68 and Batesville would be behind and time would be running out. You know, 'Ten seconds, nine, eight. Michael Menser has the ball. Seven, six, five . . . Menser shoots . . .' He would take a long shot and if he made it Batesville would win. But we rigged the game. If he didn't hit the basket he got foul shots, and if he just made one foul shot there'd be overtime and we'd do the whole thing again and he'd take another long shot. We'd fix it so that every way it turned out Michael Menser would win the game for Batesville."

Michael grew taller after junior high, but not that much heavier. Just inside the gym doors Batesville's cheerleaders were holding a large paper Batesville Bulldog, which the players were about to break through as they charged from the dressing room to play Milan. "Michael will not be first out," said Jenny Menser. "Michael has never run through the paper first because they're afraid he might not break it. Wouldn't that be embarrassing? Hitting the paper and falling back."

Michael came out last. But once the game began he was the team leader. His mother, wearing a sweatshirt covered with assorted Batesville Bulldogs buttons, sounded more like a coach than the mythical play-by-play announcer she used to be.

"Protect the ball" — a cry directed at her son, who had the basketball batted away from him momentarily.

"Play 'D.' Help out. Help out.

"Pick 'im up."

Jim Menser sat up in back with Sherman Dillard, who had already signed Menser to be point guard next season at Indiana State. Dillard had gone out of his way, driving from Terre Haute to Batesville, although it wasn't necessary. Jim Menser had told him, "Don't feel as though you have to come. Hey, go recruit some big guys."

Big Ten schools had passed on Michael because of his lack of size. Wisconsin had taken a long look, but in the end settled on a long letter to the Mensers explaining why it wasn't going to offer a scholarship. Jim was impressed with the courtesy, although it contained no surprise. Michael didn't weigh enough. "They said they couldn't imagine him playing some Purdue guard who was six two, 220 pounds," said Jim Menser. A friend of Bob Knight related that the coach told him that Menser would have been in an Indiana uniform had he been six two, because he would have been a little heavier and been able to add enough weight with the Indiana training regimen. As it was, Knight envisioned Menser sitting on the Indiana bench for at least three years. Menser was happy with Indiana State. His sister, Angie, a track and cross-country runner, already was there and liking it. She'd watch out for her little brother. Others in Batesville reasoned that if Indiana State was good enough for Larry Bird, it would be good enough for Michael Menser.

"It will be a great fit for Michael," said Jim Menser.

So with Menser and Dillard chatting quietly, and Jenny Menser all but leading the cheers several rows below, Batesville won its sixth straight game by overwhelming Milan, 87–61. Afterward, Randy Combs sat alone in an aisle between lockers in the visitors' dressing room. He was anguished but perked up to say: "It's not the worst thing to lose to Michael Menser. He's worked for everything he's gotten. We'll be okay."

"I wish I had him already," Sherman Dillard said of Menser. The thought would shorten his drive on the roads west to Terre Haute.

Far to the north in this vertical state it was much colder. Darkness had obliterated the afternoon early in "The Region," well before the Merrillville varsity and junior varsity climbed aboard a yellow school bus. They were bound for Valparaiso. Everyone called it Valpo.

Jim East's team remained a puzzle to him. He seemed to have no idea where his next problem would come from, only that there would be problems.

A week before the season Jamaal Davis had fainted during a first-period class. He'd undergone a complete physical, even worn a heart monitor to school, but no problem had been detected. Everyone was relieved, but understandably he had to miss several days of practice. That threw off East's schedule.

The coach also was worried about his players academically. He said that some had grown up in the elementary schools of Gary and were finding classroom demands at Merrillville difficult. He preached to them about studying. "I'm trying to keep them all eligible," he said.

Full of doubts, but with a coaching record suggesting he could overcome difficulties, East did all he could to prepare his team for its opening game. The night arrived, but at the appointed time, Davis didn't. The team's main hope — the team captain — was, however briefly, missing. East wondered if this was going to be a season like the previous one with Davis, when the coach had to suspend him for shouting at him.

"They're supposed to be back here at school at six and he walks in at six twenty-two," said East. "His explanation was kind of feeble. I told him, 'I really didn't have a perfect afternoon, either, when I got home from school. What's going to happen at Purdue if you do this? They'll sit you games or run you till you won't do it again.'

"So I start off my season with my star player on the bench." But he didn't sit long. "I put him in with three and a half minutes to go in the first quarter because one starter got two fouls. I didn't want to put him in that soon." It was not a good beginning; Merrillville lost on its home court and fell from the top five in preseason polls to the top fifteen. East wouldn't soon forget the upset defeat. "The losses," he said, "hang heavy in your mind."

The heaviest had been 58–57 to Steve Witty's Ben Davis team in the 1995 state championship game. East thought his Pirates were going to win — and against the best of all Ben Davis teams. Merrillville was down by two points with a minute remaining when East called time and set up a play for his best shooter, who had made five three-pointers in the game. East paused in the retelling, then rubbed his neck. With a wince he said, "The pass went right through his hands."

He was staring as if seeing the play again.

"This team is not as talented as that one," he said of his current Pirates. "I don't think we're championship contenders. I don't feel it. I just don't feel it. But Steve Witty feels it."

As much as East wanted back on the mountaintop of Indiana high school basketball, this unglamorous December night held little promise of an impending climb. "Before games you'd think I could spend my time thinking about the opponent," he said, "but instead I'm worrying about all my players just getting to the game." With everyone finally assembled he gave a small lecture to his players on being prompt. Then he turned to worrying why the bus was late. And when a yellow school bus finally showed up he stood in the bitter darkness watching the tall, heavily clothed figures get on board for Valpo.

"Let's go. We're late," he told the driver from the right-front seat.

The bus lurched. Its front doors rattled, to East's annoyance —

he asked the driver if it weren't possible to get a better bus. Everyone bounced. But not for long. It was shortly after 5 P.M., rush hour, and even the driver's back route out of Merrillville left the bus at a standstill behind a line of cars on a single-lane road. Over their right shoulders shone a planetary glow from the suburban sprawl of Merrillville — strip malls, chain restaurants, gas stations, and motels radiating from the gridlocked intersection of Broadway and U.S. 30. "Wouldn't want to have gone that way," someone offering consolation said from somewhere back in the bus. East checked his watch. Then he saw a light that made him forget temporarily that they were late and stuck in traffic.

"Look at that," he said. "That guy's combining beans. Here it is December twentieth and that guy's trying to get his beans."

A man driving a combine with a light atop it was sweeping across one of the last fields of Merrillville. A man alone in his snow-covered bean field, at that moment moving faster than every piece of automotive machinery whose headlights bounded his square of earth. How many more years could the farmer stave off the momentum of suburbia that had devoured this chunk of the state right up to his wire fence?

The Valparaiso people were waiting at the doors when the bus pulled up because time for the junior varsity game was nearing.

"Where you been?"

"Traffic. . . . Let's go, guys. Get inside."

Valparaiso's coach, Bob Punter, and East shared the rare misery of making it to the state championship game only to lose. It had happened to Valpo the year before it happened to Merillville. South Bend Clay beat Valpo, 93–88, in overtime. "I'm not over it yet," said Punter, echoing East's words. But he hadn't lost a sense of humor. Someone asked how he planned to defend Jamaal Davis, and Punter replied, "I've got a five-eight guy to stand on the shoulders of a six-five guy."

Merrillville attracted a good number of followers, among them Jerry McCory, the former police chief of Merrillville who now worked for a local utility company. He expressed confidence in his friend East. "I don't think a young coach could take this team very far. But I think he can take this team to Indianapolis again."

"I'm very skeptical," said Tom Feeney, a Merrillville High math teacher. He said the Merrillville team simply didn't compare with great Indiana teams he'd seen. His prime example was the undefeated 1971 East Chicago Washington team that included Tim Stoddard, Junior Bridgeman, and Pete Trgovich. Many consider that the best team in the history of Indiana basketball.

Feeney and another man agreed on Indiana's all-time "best" high school players.

"Best pure shooter?"

"Mount."

"Best overall?"

"Oscar."

That was Indiana. People sat and talked basketball.

John Davis, Jamaal's father, was sitting up higher. He had played on the 1970 East Chicago Roosevelt team, also undefeated, which he said firmly was better than the 1971 East Chicago Washington team. As for the current Merrillville team, it lacked "size and experience" but there was "still hope." He had two sons on the team, the younger one being the fifteen-year-old John, a sophomore reserve, six feet four and growing. "John's going to be a force to be reckoned with," the father said. "I think he's going to be six nine."

The father did not say what both East and John's mother later did. Young John simply didn't care that much about the game — not yet, at least.

East said that for the first time in Merrillville's history he was going to start an all-black five. The growing number of black players merely reflected the school's increasing proportion of African-American students. Like European ethnics before them, blacks were moving south out of Gary and its environs. In fleeing the city of 116,000, which ranked number one in homicides per capita among U.S. cities of more than 100,000, they were trying first to preserve their lives, as in the case of Jamaal Davis's mother, stepmother, and brother.

Merrillville played as East had predicted — erratically. But the team showed potential for a good season. Valparaiso hung close for a half, but the purple-clad Pirates asserted themselves in the third period, which ended just after Davis went high for an emphatic block that a teammate converted for an easy layup. Davis scored 17 points, 12 in the second half, and pulled down 10 rebounds in a relatively easy 51–40 victory. The sophomore Davis picked up a few minutes of playing time. Victory or not, East fumed.

"We're one man short," he said. "We're missing at small forward. We have to fill that void."

Just maybe the season would be long enough to give John Davis time to grow into the job, to mature. But would he?

A player called out to East from the back of the locker room. Almost everyone was on the bus. The player held up most of a uniform and a player's basketball shoes that someone had left behind. East looked it over. The stuff was marked with the number 22. "Get John back here," called East.

John Davis came back down the hall, sauntering.

"John. John . . ." East stammered. But he thought better of saying more. He yanked down his fedora and headed outside.

The good news in Anderson was something more than an easy victory over Lafayette Jefferson — a perennial power almost always referred to as Lafayette Jeff. With Eric Bush stealing, passing, and scoring, Anderson broke on top 13–2, led 45–18 at the half, and won 78–50. The bigger news was that for the first time Hecklinski had been able to coach dressed in something other than a sweatsuit. The swelling in his midsection had gone down enough for him to appear on the sidelines in conventional clothing — he chose a turtleneck and finely checked slacks. The slacks belonged to Johnny Wilson, who had a slightly larger waist size.

A few days after that game Hecklinski sat and talked with Wilson and Terry Turner, junior varsity coach Kyle Hobbs, and a volunteer assistant, Tom Champion. The five were concerned that the players hadn't been intense enough at practice on the eve of a game with rival Anderson Highland. "We're five and one because of spurts," said Hecklinski. "We haven't been intense for whole games. We don't have a stud who's going to step up and take over."

Johnny Wilson said the team lacked "a guy who gets everybody playing every night. Every night you're playing you should blow 'em right out of the gym."

The group sounded variations on the same theme, one that's even been put to music: What's the matter with kids today?

Wilson: "You've got to work hard in practice to do it in the game. I used to run all out in wind sprints. Every night at practice I'd be first because that's the way it should have been, I was the fastest on the team. Carl Erskine was always second in the sprints because he was the second fastest on the team." That would be the Carl Erskine, the Brooklyn Dodgers pitcher, one of "The Boys of Summer," and a onetime Anderson High basketball player.

Hecklinski: "These kids need inner personal drive. Trying to get kids to have that inner personal drive is so difficult." He hit his desktop — with his good right hand. His left still didn't have complete feeling in it.

Turner: "God gifted them. You don't think that speed was grown. Then we brought them in here as fifteen-year-olds and we handed them all the glory. They never paid the price for nothing."

Hecklinski: "I'm not sure this team will ever be a team that can overcome great adversity. They've never had to struggle. They should want to win. They should want to win everything."

Turner: "They don't come together on the floor in times of crisis. When have you seen 'em get together out there?"

Hecklinski: "If we lose tomorrow night I won't be surprised. If we win it'd throw my thinking in the trash. No it won't either. Because you don't know what kids today are going to do."

Wilson: "All of this has been coming the last ten years, this complete reversal, kids' attitudes. They're not like Bird."

Turner: "And Magic."

Wilson: "Magic just played. Bird would dive. Here's a guy making millions and he'd dive for the ball and risk hitting the seats."

Hecklinski: "I know how to do it. I know how to get to these kids. Sit 'em. You gotta have the balls to sit 'em a game. Sit 'em two or three games. I got the balls to do it." Pause. "I may not have the balls to do it tomorrow night."

Hobbs: "Aaron Boyd might be a leader. He starts practice up."

Hecklinski: "Maybe I'm expecting too much."

Wilson: "I don't think you're expecting too much."

Hecklinski: "If we had a practice like that ten years ago they'd be tossed out of the gym. Or I'd have 'em runnin' all night."

Turner: "January will be the time to see if we grow up as a team."

Hecklinski: "I used to like practice. Is there anything wrong with liking practice? We had *practices*. Knockdown tough. I used to love just to get to the games. These kids, they don't set goals for themselves. If we were going to play New Prairie I'd be thinking of getting twenty. If we were going to play South Bend Adams I'd just try to guard somebody. These kids, they don't set goals for themselves. Damn, I want to get out there and get ten rebounds." He waved a scouting report on Anderson Highland. "Not one will sit down and pick this up and read it."

Turner: "Who will know what number Pinkerton is?" That was Highland's Jake Pinkerton.

Wilson: "Kids just don't have that desire to be the best, to try to be the best. We didn't have water when I grew up. We had to go get water for Mom to cook."

Hecklinski: "They won't do their own homework. Now they

get driven to school. Terry, bet you had to get up and milk the cows."

Turner: "No, I didn't have to milk 'em. But I had to get up at four-thirty and do chores."

Hecklinski: "We do care about the kids. We want them to do well. Not all coaches can say that. Hey, we're good because we care. Maybe something we do will help a kid, if the kid wants to be helped. All kids have good in them, I think."

Wilson: "That's the best thing, when some kid comes back and says, 'Thanks, Coach, for making me do that. Thank you.'"

Turner: "So what did we accomplish here?"

Hecklinski: "We're going to go home and feel better because we talked."

The next night Anderson crushed Highland, 85–62.

8

Native Sons

J AMES DEAN. The name means Hollywood, spontaneous stardom, misunderstood youth — slouched and moody, collar up, cigarette dangling.

But the name James Dean also means Indiana. Before he became an American fifties icon he led a stunningly simpler life. Before he raced cars — he was on his way to a race when he died in a crash in California — he shot baskets at a hoop inside a barn. He was a better-than-decent Indiana high school basketball player. He came from the heart of the state, the prairie down 26 West from I-69 between Anderson and Fort Wayne. He came from unhurried Fairmount.

Dean grew up on a farm, though he liked being away from it. Almost daily he stayed late at Fairmount High for school activities. He was Adeline Mart Nall's prize drama student. He lettered in three sports. He was a better basketball player than he might appear in dated pictures of him in uniform, usually wearing glasses. At the end of his senior year, in 1949, he played three outstanding games in the tournament sectional, leading Fairmount to upsets over Van Buren and Mississinewa before a loss to Marion. A quick-enough guard, he scored a total of 40 points in the three games.

Fairmount High is now a middle school in the heart of town. The high school is called Madison-Grant. Madison-Grant had a player named Kyle Runyan whose name was mentioned more often by the townspeople than James Dean's. It was visitors who wanted to talk about Dean. Wasn't it somewhere around here that Dean had played ball?

A hoop used by James Dean — in town he was called Jim or Jimmy — still hangs in the barn of a cattle farm out on the seldom-traveled Sand Pike Road. Marcus and Ortense Winslow raised their nephew Jim there. He was born in Marion, but they took him in after his mother died when he was nine and his father moved to California. It was young Marc's farm now. He said that it was fine if someone wanted to come by that day and see the hoop, but that he had to go someplace. The barn was unlocked. Feel free to roam, he said, just don't smoke in the barn. Such was Hoosier hospitality.

You could raise the latch, slide the barn door to the right, and walk into the hayloft. Cattle stirred in the depths below the loft's rough wood floor. A rusted black hoop remained just a few feet inside. Dean was like all the Indiana farm boys who hung baskets in barns. The hoop had a chain net, which Marc had said was added after Dean played there. Dean was older than Marc and used to throw in shots over him. A photograph of Dean in the down-town gallery catches him in the midst of a half hook shot at that very spot in the barn. That was before he looked moody.

Now Dean lies in Park Cemetery, down the road from the farm. Three young women were standing at his grave on this cold December day. A plain rose-colored monument: "James B. Dean 1931-1955." People come from around the world to stand there, from France, from Japan, from California. Someone had left a red rose on top of the monument.

Adeline Nall was buried nearby. She had died only recently, at age ninety. Steve Patterson, in the *Chronicle-Tribune*, of nearby Marion, her birthplace as well as Dean's, wrote this lead with a Fairmount dateline: "By now, Adeline Mart Nall has had her little talk with James Dean."

The writer then quotes Nall from a 1974 interview: "I remember one time when Jim was in high school, and we were staging a play and I cast him as an old man. He came to me and said, 'Mrs. Nall, you don't know anything about casting; I'm a perfect juvenile.'

"When I get to heaven, I'm going to say, 'Jim, look what you did in *Giant*. Do you still think I don't know anything about casting?' "

Giant was the movie in which he played a man who aged and became gray. *Giant* came after *Rebel Without a Cause*, which came after *East of Eden*, which all came after Adeline Nall. For six years in junior and senior high school she taught Dean literature, Spanish, math, and speech. He offered her a cigarette once in class, and she had to restrain herself, as she put it, from "popping him."

In his senior year she coached him in a dramatic monologue from a novel by Charles Dickens, and he won the state title. She took him by train to Colorado, where he competed in the National Forensic League finals. He finished sixth.

"When he'd be drying dishes for me, Jimmy used to dream out loud about getting in the movies," Nall once said. "Course I didn't pay any attention — figured that'd be impossible for an Indiana farm boy.

"There wasn't anything very different about him — except that he had this strange ability to take you along with his feelings. When something would go wrong at school or on one of his ball teams, we'd all feel blue until he came out of it."

The end came on September 30, 1955, with a crash on a road

near Paso Robles. Dean in his new silver-colored 550 Porsche Spyder collided at an intersection with another car. Bill Hickman, possibly Dean's best friend in Hollywood, was following, and saw a cloud of smoke. He pulled Dean from the wreckage. He'd been hurrying to Salinas to rest up for a race he was entered in the next day. By then auto racing was his sport. But he was dead at the age of twenty-four.

Bob Pulley was one of Dean's best friends in Fairmount, when Dean cared more about basketball. Pulley was one of his pallbearers. All six men who carried Dean to his Sand Pike Road grave came from Fairmount or close by. Pulley, now sixty-six, lived in a white farmhouse across open land from Madison-Grant High. Late one afternoon he was on a ladder stringing Christmas lights on his house. He said that each year he puts more than 15,000 lights on his property. In the vast open space you would see the house for miles. Now the sun was setting and it was growing colder.

Pulley wore boots and a cap and layers of clothing covered finally by a one-piece olive-drab wool farm suit. He invited a visitor into his barn to talk. He had a portable heater going. Right off, he said how sorry he was that the single tournament was in jeopardy. "We used to go in a blizzard to another town to see a ball game." To see Jim play.

"He was fast and good," said Pulley. "He was a perfectionist in what he did. I'm the same way, but I wasn't as talented as he was. We'd play ice hockey out on the Winslow farm, on the pond behind the barn. His uncle played, too. We played a lot of ice hockey out there, and when it got too cold we went into the barn and played basketball."

And then: "It was sad."

Now he was talking about 1955. It was February, and Dean came home to Indiana for what would be the last time, alive.

"Jim and I always ran around together," said Pulley, "but I was hesitant to call him. But my mother said, 'Go ahead and call him.' I called him. I figured he was big time then. I was wrong. He was tickled to death. I said, 'Let's go out and party.'"

As Pulley told it, Dean paused. "What is there to do?" he responded.

Pulley reminded him: "We'll go to the Sports Bar in Marion."

Pulley explained: "We always used to go there. It's long gone. It was down on the square facing the courthouse. I said to him, 'If there's not that much going on, we'll go over to Pee-ru.' That's Peru. I call it Pee-ru."

Bob Pulley and Jim Dean went off to the Sports Bar in Marion.

Pulley recalled a man coming up to them in the bar as the only harsh incident he knew of in Dean's return home. " 'Hey, Dean, give me your autograph.' Jim obliged, and the guy just tore it up in front of us."

Pulley kept the autograph Jim gave him. But: "I've been offered up to $7,000 for it. I'm trying to get $12,000 out of it. Probably will. It's not eatin' nothin'."

Pulley hadn't been over to the high school to watch Kyle Runyan, a six five senior and one of the better players in the state. Pulley said he didn't go to the games anymore, but that his wife, Shirley, still did and was at the school preparing food in the cafeteria for fans. Almost every school in Indiana offered something special on game nights, and Madison-Grant put on a big pregame feed for just a few dollars. Steaks were the pride, but Pulley's wife had told him they'd sold out the night before when Madison-Grant beat Blackford. "You'll have to eat something else," he said. The school was a two-minute drive. In a parking lot in back were several cars parked with people in them, mostly older couples. They were waiting for the school doors to open and the food to be served at six o'clock, and at precisely six o'clock almost everyone got out of their cars and quick-stepped against the wind and into the building. The homemade vegetable soup felt like a godsend.

Later you could settle in with a bag of popcorn. Popcorn was the uniform treat at games in Indiana. A sign at the front of

Madison-Grant's gym: "No food or drink in the gym except popcorn."

Madison-Grant jumped to a 38–10 lead over Lapel before a spectator could get to the bottom of a bag.

Runyan scored seventeen in the 91–56 victory. He played with a back brace because he'd hurt himself his junior year playing on the football team as a wide receiver and tight end. His interests would have been better served had he skipped football, with its risks of injury, and concentrated on the sport that would earn him a college scholarship. But he seemed devoid of ego and committed to the success of Madison-Grant. "It's a small school," he explained, "and you play more than one sport."

He gave the impression of one who might be completely happy taking over the family pig farm if he never made it as a famous player in the big cities. Dean had wanted to get away, but still Adeline Nall had said: "The feel of Indiana soil under his feet was the source of much of his strength."

Jackie Robinson and Jimmy Erskine . . .

The two names stirred feelings in the white-haired man seated across the desk. They were the names of those who taught him love, instilled a wonder, and fueled an energy still burning as he turned seventy. Jackie was his friend, Jimmy his son.

Carl Erskine was welcomed to the Brooklyn Dodgers by Jackie Robinson. Robinson's hand was out when Erskine walked into the Brooklyn clubhouse in 1948. From where did that generosity arise in a black man being persecuted for breaking baseball's color barrier? "I knew you'd be coming up when I saw you in spring training," Robinson told him. Robinson thought of Erskine as a teammate, just as Erskine thought of him.

Jimmy Erskine was born April 1, 1960, Carl and Betty Erskine's fourth child. He was a Down's syndrome child at a time when much of society preferred to look away from life's challenged people. But Carl welcomed Jimmy's arrival as warmly as Jackie had welcomed him to the big leagues. Carl's life had been grounded on reason and unselfishness.

Jimmy was born only months after his father had retired from the Dodgers. Carl had planned on working for a shirt manufacturer in New York and settling in the suburbs, but he wanted Jimmy to grow up in the best place he knew, and that was the place where he'd grown up. He took Betty and the children — Susan, Gary, Danny, and Jimmy — home to Anderson, Indiana.

Anderson is where Roger Kahn came to visit in the early seventies when he wrote about Carl and Jimmy in *The Boys of Summer*. Jimmy was nine. Now in his mid-thirties Jimmy still was making advances in a life Carl happily shared each day. The son drew a modest paycheck doing a variety of jobs at a sheltered workshop, the Hopewell Center; the father usually drove him to work in the mornings and back home again in the afternoons.

Erskine, vice chairman of the Star Financial Bank in Anderson, also was trying to apply his life's experiences to the change troubling many people in Anderson — the closing of the Anderson High building and the elimination of the Madison Heights name. He belonged to "The Committee of 95," a group of businessmen, most of whom had a long-range vision of a single modern high school. Another group, "Save Our Schools," was battling to keep all three high schools. "What's helped me understand a little bit about change is that I've been through several changes," he said.

He'd come home, brushed up on math and English at Anderson University as a thirty-two-year-old freshman, worked as an insurance agent and coached baseball at the university, accepted a job offer from the bank, made its board, and become its president. He'd seen Anderson suffer through what residents there called "the auto depression" in the late seventies and early eighties. At one point unemployment had shot up to 20.9 percent as companies that manufactured auto parts laid off workers. And then he'd seen the town recover. He'd seen baseball change as well. "Baseball was a day game. It went to night during my time. It was a train game. It went to airlines. It was a radio game. Radio's still there, but TV's the big thing. It went from East Coast to West Coast. I could never imagine that I'd be wearing a uniform that said Dodgers playing in a different city. Well, once I went through that I got conditioned a little bit. You do survive, and sometimes it's better."

What was baseball's best change during his time?

Without hesitation: "It went from all-white to integrated."

There was nothing fancy about Erskine. His bank office was windowless. He had on a green sports jacket and striped green tie. A large color photo, framed but yet to be hung, was propped against a wall. It was taken in daylight at Ebbets Field: the "Boys of Summer" at the batting cage. Erskine was the man in the middle. Left to right: Pee Wee Reese, Carl Furillo, Jackie, Erskine, Gil Hodges, Don Newcombe, Duke Snider, Roy Campanella. The symmetry: Robinson toward the left of the frame, right hand on hip; Hodges toward the right, left hand on hip. Erskine between them, with a bat held almost vertically, grasped loosely at both the handle and the barrel. "I don't remember the picture being taken," he said. "I must have been pitching that day. That's the only reason I'd be out there for batting practice."

The photograph — with Jackie and Newk and Campy in it — catches the momentous but late change in the game. Too late for Johnny Wilson — Erskine's Anderson High teammate — as it was too late for other great black ballplayers. "You know how people familiar with Jackie's career at UCLA say that baseball wasn't even his best sport?" said Erskine. "Well, I'm not so sure that John Wilson wasn't a better baseball player than he was a basketball player. He played for the Chicago Americans in the black league. One day we both had games in Pittsburgh. We sat out in a park and talked about how two kids from Anderson ended up playing baseball that day in Pittsburgh."

Erskine had thought many times, If only Jackie had been allowed just to play the game instead of having the burden of pioneering. If only Johnny and he could have met up on a major league field and not on a park bench.

Erskine kept three baseballs in a glass case in his office: one from his 3–2 World Series victory over the Yankees, October 2, 1953, when he struck out a record fourteen; the ball from his no-hitter against the Cubs, June 19, 1952; and another from his no-hitter against the New York Giants, May 12, 1956. He'd also hung two photos. One was an old wire-service shot of Betty hugging him after the record-strikeout World Series game. The other showed Tommy Lasorda and Carl Erskine — and Jimmy Erskine, too — all in Dodgers uniforms at Dodgertown in Vero Beach.

"Jimmy has had this momentous time in history when people opened up to him. He's been accepted, he's been encouraged, and people have changed their views about those who are challenged," said his father. "There is so much more understanding now. I would never wish a Down's syndrome child on anyone, but I can't begin to tell you the joy that Jimmy has brought our family. He takes part in Special Olympics. He's a swimmer, he bowls. He has a job. He brings in a small amount of money. He pays taxes. He's part of society."

Sometimes he and Jimmy took in a game at the Wigwam. Erskine had been going there for years with his other children. Susan had been a cheerleader. Gary and Danny had played on the team, as had their father before them. Carl had season tickets for almost half a century. But who could say how long the Wigwam would be there when the building attached to it was being closed as part of school consolidation?

"I don't have a passion to say, 'Don't move out of that old building that I went to school in.' I mean, I love the old place. But I know the reasons. Technology and other reasons. But it would bother me if there wasn't going to be an Anderson High School anymore. I really wanted us to keep Anderson High School. It's appropriate, I think. And I think in the long run we can be best served with one school, state-of-the-art. Anderson's going through a lot of changes with GM downsizing, our population decreasing some. We want people to move to Anderson and send their children to school here.''

As for the change Hoosiers state-wide were discussing, Erskine had his mind made up: ''What of tradition do you keep and what do you leave behind? This has been a classic debate since man started breathing. I'm hooked on a tradition of a single-class tournament in Indiana because to me we live in a subsidized age. We look to government and other sources to subsidize almost anything so that it appears to be something it isn't. To make it more palatable. To have less of the old harshness of life, that you either win or lose.

''Years ago it was such a prize to get a first-place ribbon of some kind. As a kid growing up you didn't get a lot of awards. Only if you really succeeded you got honored for it. By the time my kids came along there was change. One time they came home from a bowling tournament and they had a big trophy and I said, man, what'd you do, win the city championship? No, we finished fifth.

''People my age, maybe a little older, who went through the Depression and a lot of hardships, don't want our kids to suffer. We don't want them to have bad experiences. Somehow that thinking got to the point where we don't want our kids to be defeated. But in the real world a person has to perform. No one says we're going to make it easier so you can look better. What's happened with multi-class basketball is that people are frustrated because the percentages are small of making it through to the championship. Okay, the school that wins in its class ought to be proud. But it is not my concept of the championship.''

In 1944 Johnny Wilson and Carl Erskine almost led Anderson to a state championship. But Wilson, a sophomore then, had injured his back when he had his legs taken out from under him and he crashed to the floor during the victory that put Anderson into the final four. The next week he could barely make it up and down the court, and Erskine fouled out for the only time as a high school player; Anderson lost by two points to Kokomo. Johnny got the job done in '46, when he led Anderson to the state title. By then Carl was in the Dodgers' minor league organization. These days, they still meet up at the Wigwam.

One evening before a game, Carl talked of his love for Anderson's basketball teams and how a Chicago Cubs scout had found him when he was a fifteen-year-old sophomore and tried to sign him. "I didn't sign because it just didn't feel right," he said. "I would no longer be eligible for high school sports. I would no longer be an Indian basketball player. You know, when I was walking along the edge of the court a few minutes ago I wanted to turn and dribble once or twice. I don't think getting a Dodger uniform was any bigger a thrill than when Charlie Cummings gave me a varsity uniform with an Indian."

Carl had on a red sweater, blending with all the people in the stands wearing something red or green for the home team. At the half and one other time, Jimmy wanted to go to the lobby, to a concession stand or a men's room, and Carl took his son's hand as they climbed down the steps. Once, a man caught Carl's attention, and as the two exchanged greetings Jimmy slipped away. Carl kept talking a moment, then hurried to catch up with Jimmy. Carl was smiling. He was moving like a young man.

9

Quadruple-
header

NINE A.M. on Saturday, December 28, and the traffic into New Castle already was heavy. It was moving, though, because Route 3 is no ordinary state road. It's a dual highway built to accommodate the world's largest high school gym — and that gym already was filling for the season's first big day of basketball. Four ranked teams, four games: 10 A.M. and noon, a consolation game at 6 P.M., the winners going for glory and a trophy at 8. It was the twentieth Indiana Basketball Hall of Fame Classic. A classic it would be.

The small schools, Batesville, winner of its first seven games and up to number nine in the media poll, and Madison-Grant, 6–1 and number seventeen, would open at 10. Fifth-ranked DeKalb, 7–0, with Recker off to a 32-point scoring average, and sixth-ranked Anderson, 7–1, would meet in a showdown worthy of the starting time, high noon. The format imitated that of the tournament regionals, semistates, and final four: a team was asked to win twice in one day. In addition the format was designed to put a small school in the final game. The game of games figured to be the big boys, DeKalb-Anderson. Big teams with big dreams.

The setting, New Castle's Chrysler Fieldhouse, was impressive. When Kent Benson, Indiana's "Mr. Basketball" of 1973, and Steve Alford, "Mr. Basketball" 1983, played for New Castle High, the temporary seats always were up to increase capacity to 9,314. The arena is a sunken bowl with twenty-four rows of thick hardwood benches overlooking a parquet floor. A field house of dreams.

It's breathtaking when it's empty and you can stand on the parquet and look up at the perfect spacing between rows, and the benches brought to a high gloss. You feel you're in a building as precious as any fine theater. But it's even more impressive when it's filled with people and the game means not much tangibly but just about everything to everybody in the building, especially to an Indiana kid who is playing.

Well-known players have put on memorable performances in this Christmas holiday event, among them Damon Bailey, Shawn Kemp, Eric Montross, Alford, and Glenn Robinson. A name would emerge this day to rank among them. It was a day that spectators said felt like a tournament regional because it was balmy for December, as tournament time could be in March. And more: people were bringing a degree of anticipation for a high school basketball event that seemed rare.

When Menser and Batesville lined up against Kyle Runyan and Madison-Grant to begin this quadruple-header, you could smell the morning coffee and see people's excitement — their knees moving up and down anxiously, hands clenched, voices already raised. You had to remind yourself this was not Chicago or New York, not the Bulls and the Knicks. It was high school basketball in New Castle, Indiana, on a Saturday morning.

Game one was spectacular enough, yet only the warm-up.

Menser and Runyan traded baskets and led their teams. At the half it was 27–25, Batesville. After three quarters it was 39–37, Batesville. The game was as tense as the score was close, and everyone could hardly wait for the final eight minutes. It was then that Batesville played up to its coach's confidence. Melvin Siefert had said this team had poise and stamina, and it did. Batesville stepped up its man-to-man pressure defense, dominated the rebounding, kept running. And because it was the fourth quarter, it was Menser's time.

Little Menser stole the ball at one end, saved it from going out of bounds off a teammate at the other end, turned and whipped a pass to another teammate for a layup. The wizardry seemed to mesmerize Madison-Grant as Batesville moved on to win comfortably, 59–43. Menser scored 19, Runyan 17. Madison-Grant's coach, Terry Martin, a large, calm man, said that Batesville's "quickness" made the difference. Small-town teams in Indiana usually like to slow the tempo, but Batesville could play deliberately or quickly. Leaving for the team's motel to plan his strategy for the championship game, Siefert said Batesville could do better yet. "We didn't play up to our ability," he said.

At ten minutes before noon all the seats were taken and people were standing in the back awaiting Anderson and DeKalb.

DeKalb's Cliff Hawkins had had his Barons pointing to this game since the preseason.

Anderson's Ron Hecklinski couldn't be sure of a team leader or much else as he addressed his players minutes before the tap. "Look at this word I've put on this board," he said. "It's as important as anything. 'Communicate.' 'Communicate.' Now get out there and play hard, because you're the best team. But you know what? Sometimes the best team doesn't always get it done because they don't compete. You get out there and you compete. I hear all the Indian stuff as you walk out, and I love that. But I hope it's from the heart. I hope it's from the heart. I hope you really believe that. I hope you really believe that."

Then, quietly, he went on, "In the name of the Father, and of the Son, and of the Holy Spirit, amen. Dear Lord, first of all we want to thank you for giving us the courage, the strength, and the ability to be participating in this game today. We ask that we represent Anderson High School in the highest fashion, we ask that no one be injured, and we ask that everyone come out and play as hard as they can today. Thank you for everything this year. It's been a wonderful year, and as we head into the new year continue to be with us, Lord. In the name of the Father, and of the Son, and of the Holy Spirit, amen."

Hecklinski continued, "Now let's do it. You play the way the Indians play. You play with heart, you play with courage, and you play with desire. Now go out there and leave your skin on this floor."

They ran out the door so fast you thought they might miss the floor altogether.

Recker, who had warmed up for this game with 49 points against Fort Wayne Snider, stepped up to jump for DeKalb, and the action was under way. Four minutes into it the noise was remarkable — the place sounded like a tunnel with a train coming through.

Hawkins was stamping in front of the DeKalb bench, and Hecklinski had edged onto the court to raise referee baiting to a new dimension: "I just had a transplant. I can't get this worked up, and it's your fault," he shouted at an official.

The official laughed. It was 15-all at the quarter.

In the second quarter Eric Bush stole the ball from Recker, drove, and scored to put Anderson ahead 18–15. A few plays later, Recker stole the ball from Bush and fed a teammate to make it 21–18, DeKalb.

Recker hit a three-pointer. But he was shooting excessively from long range, and he was missing more than he was making. Still, DeKalb held a sizable margin at the half, 33–26. The crowd roar lowered to a hum of talk. Anderson's players trudged to the locker room and slumped on benches. Hecklinski took no time for prayer.

"You're playing scared shitless out there. You missed the rim on two shots. You're playing tentative. You guys intimidated by DeKalb? If DeKalb intimidates you there's going to be some other schools that are going to flat intimidate you. You gotta be kiddin' me. If you don't have a shot get your feet set and move the ball. If you have a shot, get your feet set and take it. And this is killin' you right here. How many transition baskets they got? Probably six or seven. Everybody's so damn afraid of Recker it's not even funny. You're afraid of him. Go up and make the layup. Recker won't stop you.

"I got news for you. If you think that he's going to the Big Ten and tear everybody up in the Big Ten, think again. Anybody that comes down and has the freedom to take those crazy shots like he has he ought to score thirty points a game. But you guys are intimidated by him. You get the ball inside all day long and he ain't touchin' it inside. Get the ball inside. Move the ball, screen, and cut, and take good shots. And quit bein' intimidated against that old stupid-ass zone. Two-three zone. You're all standin' around."

He sputtered, twice failing to get out the next words. He tried a collegial warning: "Unless you turn it up, you're in the consolation game. I'm just tellin' ya." Then he swung back to anger.

"Who was supposed to block out thirty-two that time?"

A player replied, quietly, "I had 'im. He just went over my back."

Hecklinski continued, "They can go over our backs. We can't go over theirs, then. Wait a minute. Let me hear the reason we're four for eleven from the free-throw line. You say, 'I had him on the block out.' You say, 'He hit my hand on the air ball.' Gimme why we're four for eleven from the free-throw line. The ball sucks? I don't want to hear excuses.

"On that little two-three zone, get in the gaps and attack it. And hit the boards."

Moving to the blackboard, he said, "This is it and this is it.

You know what . . . and I'm not even that smart . . . these are the two biggest points in this game: rebounding and transition 'D.' They're excited to play you. And they want the chance to take you out. They really do. And the way you're playing they're gonna take you out. You're not playing smart. You're playing tentative and you're not doing these two things."

"Three and a half minutes, Coach."

"As slow as we're playin' it'll take us three minutes to get down the steps. Now play hard and attack. Quit tiptoeing around. And play smart. You're all a bunch of veterans. You've all played before. Let's get after this thing."

Immediately, Recker hurt Hecklinski's credibility. To open the second half he stuffed a shot at the end of a fast break and added a layup to put DeKalb ahead 38−26. But after that he was inconsistent and Anderson's players seemed to remember the logical points Hecklinski had made at halftime. They split the zone and made good shots, and Bush played like a leader — he distributed passes, and, like that, Anderson pulled into a tie at 41.

People were craning, hardly anyone was sitting for long. What basketball game could surpass the fury on the floor in this one?

And then Recker took over. He outscored Anderson 11−2. He put DeKalb ahead 52−43 with 6:45 to play. He played big: big leaps, big strides. And one big shot. He hit from 35 feet. He hung in the air before letting go. It was a preposterously long shot and a gasp went up from the crowd.

He made the shot — but he was playing out of control. And Anderson battled back. Bush tied the score at 56 on a 15-footer. With 1:45 remaining, Recker elected to take another three-pointer. It missed. Anderson stalled. DeKalb's reserves all stood, wanting this game. But with 34 seconds left Bush penetrated and fed six-five junior center Duane Miller underneath for the winning basket. Recker fired up two desperation three-point attempts in the last six seconds and it was over. Anderson had finished with a 16−4 run and the victory, 59−56.

Anderson won because of its balanced attack. Four players scored in double figures. Recker scored 31 for DeKalb. But he connected on only 11 of 28 shots, and only three of 12 on three-point attempts. And he kicked a chair in frustration moments after the game had ended.

It was not the kind of behavior Indiana fans expected from a potential "Mr. Basketball," and people chatting on the Internet in days to come would suggest that Recker was self-centered for taking so many shots and ill-mannered on top of it. The consensus: he'd shot DeKalb into the game, and out of it.

Ben Davis's Steve Witty, who had attended, put it mildly several days later when he said, "I would have had a little better shot selection."

Everyone had watched Recker's every move. It probably was the most pressurized situation of his life to that point.

An advertisement in the event's program for two all-star games in the spring began: "Come see Luke Recker . . ."

In the pall of defeat, Hawkins had to deal with a contingent of inquisitive reporters.

"My feeling was Luke got us rolling at the end of the third quarter. The problem was that he continued to play with that kind of emotion when what we needed to do was pass the ball and work it a little bit. . . . But what really disappointed me was when we had I think fifteen seconds to go or so and he had the ball and Nate [Brown] was wide open on the right side and had he gone ahead and upped it to Nate, posted low, got the ball, then I think he would have made that shot, you know, for sure. Almost for sure . . .

"I think he got caught in the emotion. I think more than anything he got caught in the idea, 'I have to do this for the Barons.' Luke took it all on himself to try to win the basketball game when we needed to work a little bit harder as a unit. That's something he'll understand and that's something we'll learn from this.

"For nine months we wanted to win this thing, and so tonight with the consolation game this is going to be very, very difficult because emotionally we're going to have some problems."

Recker stood at the doorway. He wore a red Indiana cap backward and a sad look. "Shot selection," he said. "I had a lot to do with it. We've got to learn not to get caught up in the hype of the game and just take the shot that comes to us. We're very, very, very disappointed."

Many of the fans stayed put during the afternoon, eating barbecue in an adjoining room and talking basketball. That would give them a full twelve hours in the gym.

Meanwhile, Batesville scrambled to get ready for Anderson. Siefert had prepared solely to play Madison-Grant. He had had no discussion with his players about either Anderson or DeKalb. His philosophy: "You've got to keep it simple with kids. You don't want to put too many things into their heads."

Siefert took the team to dinner at Bob Evans. After that he had his players stay in their motel rooms and watch a delayed telecast of Anderson-DeKalb in its entirety. He and his staff did, too, and then they watched parts of tapes on Anderson. Siefert decided to open with a man-to-man defense, believing he would have to switch to a zone shortly because of Anderson's speed. With that he took his team back to play.

The Anderson team had gone home, just twenty miles, to have dinner at their homes and assemble again at the Wigwam for a meeting. Pam drove Ron, already weary from the day. He rested at home, but he couldn't sleep. He rejoined his players back at New Castle as they got dressed for Batesville. Hecklinski warned them of the possible upset — he'd just observed one in the making out on the floor.

There, little Madison-Grant was putting it to a dispirited DeKalb bunch, 67–59. Recker fouled out in the last minute. It was the end of a nightmare that neither he nor the rest of the team nor Hawkins would forget for weeks. Recker scored 34 points in his second game but made only 14 of 33 shots. His three-point shooting slipped to three of 14 — just six of an outlandish 26 three-point attempts for the two games. He ended his doubleheader with 65 points but he had taken 61 shots, and DeKalb in one day had lost as many games as it had the entire previous season. "He tried to take the ball game into his hands and it hurt him both games," said Madison-Grant's Runyan, who scored 19. "When we saw 'em on TV, we knew we would beat this team."

DeKalb was en route home as Hecklinski's upset warning appeared to be coming true. Anderson started its best defensive player, a reserve, on Menser, but Menser passed around him and shot over him to forge a 16–9 lead. Batesville's motion offense worked like smooth machinery.

Bush was switched to guard Menser and the two played magnificently. Menser drove and scored on Bush; Bush drove and scored on Menser. At the half it was 34–29, Batesville.

Right then a person had to wonder why anyone would want to change Indiana basketball. It already was a moral victory for Batesville. No matter the outcome, here was the beauty of the small school challenging the bigger one.

The talk from the Batesville section was, "Hey, we can play with these guys."

In the third quarter Anderson rallied to lead 43–39. But Batesville regained its momentum and managed a tie at 44. Morning had turned to afternoon and then to night. Only eight minutes remained. Menser's time.

If there was one shot that did it, it was a baseline jumper Menser fired over the top of Bush. It made the score 51–48.

But with 1:12 remaining and Batesville hanging on, 53–51, Bush stole the ball with nothing but open court ahead. A Batesville player lunged and hung on to Bush. Leaping onto the court, Hecklinski cried out for an intentional foul — two free throws and the ball. He rendered a variation on the theme he used with the official in the first game. "You know, I just had a liver transplant. And I got this real big pain in the side of my liver just now and it's all because of you that I've got this pain." This time Hecklinski drew no laugh but rather a technical foul.

Menser, naturally, converted both shots, and Batesville got to keep the ball.

Final: Batesville 62, Anderson 54. Menser had 31 points, five rebounds, three assists.

Three hundred people would be in the Batesville gym to greet the team at 1 A.M.

Hecklinski's last words of the day to his players were, "I don't know why I push myself and I can't get that kind of effort out of you guys. I don't think we did a thing different in the second half. And I don't feel bad at all about getting that technical foul. There would have been a time when I would have walked in here and felt so low for getting that, but the way you guys competed I don't feel bad at all. You didn't come out here and play with anything. You didn't come out and play with any passion or energy. You messed with the game. I had no qualm about shaking Coach's hand and telling him his team did a wonderful job because they did everything they had to beat you. They rebounded. They outcut you. They outhustled you." He paused.

"They outhustled you. That's what disappoints me the most. Because teams can make more shots, teams can do things better, but they outhustled you.

"And you know what else bothers me? I don't believe you really understand what it takes to be champion. When you get to a game like this, you put it all on the line. But not only do you play hard, you think. We were down four points and you took an NBA three. All we gotta do is drive the ball to the basket and score and we're down two with fifteen seconds left. But that wasn't the only play. What really upsets me is when I have to tell you to go and accept the second-place trophy because you were the second-best team. That's how you played and that's what you deserved.

"Don't be going through life thinking that people are going to hand you things. And don't be going through life thinking that the Batesvilles of the world don't exist and that they aren't good enough. Because, baby, they do exist. It had nothing to do with talent. Were Batesville's players better than our players? Not by a long shot. It had to do with right here, boys.''

He pointed to his head.

"And there."

He tapped his heart.

"They're a team that hustles, works. They handed it to you on a platter. It's a classic. It is a classic. I've seen it happen so many times. When I walked in this locker room before the game, I knew it. Nobody with a game face on, was there? Nobody. That's sad. That's really sad. And that's what scares me about this team. Because if that team can do it to you a lot of other teams can. And you can go home and just play it off, which you probably will. Because that's what's the matter with people today, just play it off. Go home, play it off, blame it on somebody else. But it's worth lookin' in the mirror. You missed some layups. You missed some easy shots. Not going after a rebound. My problem is the way you approached this game. That better not happen again this year.''

He walked from the room, the clack of his leather heels resounding.

As the minutes passed the players followed, one by one.

Here came Bush. He had had 14 points, six assists, five rebounds. He was half dragging his equipment bag and working a slice out of a peeled orange with his free hand. He was too crestfallen to speak. In the corridor he saw Pam Hecklinski and, still silent, walked up to her. She put her arms around him. Neither needed to say anything.

At length Bush moved on.

Famous teams, famous players lose, but none came to mind who took defeat any harder than Bush, and earlier, DeKalb. It seems almost a part of pro games for athletes to profess sorrow in a loss, and often it is genuine. But there are many more consolations at that level: a new contract, endorsements, next times. When did a professional player hurt the most? Often he'll say it was in his earlier life, after some college or high school game. Sometimes it's only after a pro athlete has completed his career and has more wealth than he needs that he has time to look back; then one might hear from him remorse that he is unfulfilled for never winning a championship, never getting a ring. On a Saturday among Indiana schoolboys winning was important and defeat hurt to the bone because youths' perspectives can narrow to a small point, as when one looks through a cone from its base to its apex. On this day their whole world was that one place. The game was the only thing.

10

Works in Progress

We're like blocks of stone, out of which
the sculptor carves the forms of men.
The blows of His chisel, which hurt us
so much, are what makes us perfect.
• William Nicholson, *Shadowlands*

ANDERSON High's Eric Bush had twice known a grief that left him uncertain and at times ambivalent about his future. He was only sixteen years old and yet on January 7, 1991, Deloris Perry, his mother, died in Anderson at the age of thirty-nine, from complications from asthma. Later that year, police knocked down the door of the family's apartment and arrested his father for drug possession. Eric was at home and witnessed the break-in. Charles Bush went to prison.

Life seemed almost as surreal to Eric when Gary and Cindy Weatherford befriended him, then became his legal guardians — a white couple offering love to a black youth. He had trouble at first understanding their generosity, that it was genuine, that he could adapt to it and accept it. They gave him hope. Because of their supervision his grades improved. He took care of basketball, developing into the starting point guard as a freshman at Anderson, and the game preoccupied him to a degree that he failed to notice his coach's health deteriorating. On the eve of his junior season when he learned that Ron Hecklinski had been taken for a liver transplant Bush belatedly realized the possible consequences for his coach. A familiar feeling came over him again, the fear of being left behind.

A visit to the hospital failed to hearten him. Hecklinski was full of tubes and could barely speak — although he pointed to a letter for Bush from a college basketball recruiter and made a small joke, "I'm getting your mail here."

The coach had been a reassuring presence to his player. Hecklinski was tall and forceful, Bush small and introverted. Bush liked it, either way, when Hecklinski would put his arm around him and be his pal, or sternly demand something more from him as a player. You could always hear Hecklinski's voice in the Wigwam, as big as the building is. In the hospital Bush sat in a chair he'd pulled close to his coach. But unsettled by the sight of the big man brought down, Bush kept his eyes on the television set as much as he could. Hecklinski in the hospital bed seemed like somebody Bush hadn't known. During the visit the coach had to have a tube to his body replaced. "Eric realized," said Gary Weatherford, "that this was really serious, not like a broken arm."

Bush went back to Anderson and shot hoops during the last days of summer and into the fall, but he couldn't help wondering whether Hecklinski would coach. After the previous season they had watched the tape of the last game, the loss to eventual state champion Ben Davis in the state's final eight. The two had agreed that if Anderson was to improve in 1996–97 Bush would have to establish himself as the team leader. To have reached the final eight with mostly sophomores was an indication of Anderson's talent; its players had, like youthful bees, swarmed their way to success without an assertive leader. "You've got to step up, Eric" — that was the coach's postseason directive.

The words seemed to fuel Bush. In the gyms of Anderson he possessed a blend of determination and skill. He went to such camps as Five-Star in Pennsylvania, but always he was happy to come home and play the game with his Anderson teammates. "Use your head. Make good decisions" — this was more of what Hecklinski had told him about how to play point guard. It was another coaching cliché, but a fundamental truth if a point guard was going to be effective. But by late September Bush had no head coach around to keep him attentive to his preparations — and to help get the other players ready. Bush was one of the best high school guards in the state, but Hecklinski was the man Bush needed most to refine his talent.

Bush did everything fast — shoot, pass, dribble — but he still had to learn to think faster than he acted. When Bush got out on a fast break with the ball anything was possible, but whatever happened would be over in a blink. Often what he did would be a cause for marvel. He was a spindly five-ten 165-pounder who could slither among taller foes for a layup, or pull up with the familiar squeak-stop of rubber on wood to fire a jump shot. Sometimes he would find an open teammate for a pass — but not often enough, in Hecklinski's view. "Sometimes Eric's idea of leadership," the coach said, "is playing one-on-five." But Bush was willing, his attitude right. He loved playing in the Wigwam: "The best feeling in the world that I have had so far," he said. Bush felt relieved when Hecklinski made it back for the season. By January he sensed the team could win the state championship and said, "I think about it every day."

Charles Bush was released on probation in March 1993 after serving two years in a Madison County correctional facility. He had five sons, four of them adults, but he was not yet ready to take responsibility for Eric. Charles lived with his mother, Daisy Fuller, and then with his stepbrother. He did little with his time. "I didn't even have any shoes," he said. "I would get shoes from my boys to wear."

Then: "Last year I was talking to my probation officer about my children, myself, and we agreed that I needed to establish myself with a place of our own, our own home, our own automobile, what we need for us. I call it putting my head on straight. I buckled down to do it. It's been a really hard struggle, financially, anyway.

"I'm staying out of trouble. I'm staying clean. By the grace of God everything's working out."

He'd gotten a job. He'd gotten a second one, and kept it. He did odd jobs at a hotel in town, seven days a week, midnight to 8 A.M. He'd missed just one day in seven months. In December 1996 he was able to rent a first-floor apartment in a small frame house in downtown Anderson. "It's taken me two and a half years just to have enough money to get myself this straight," he said. It was a bright, cold morning in January; he had just come from work and he was tired. Some days he was so tired he couldn't make it to the Wigwam for games before he had to go to work. But he hated to miss a game. "It's exhilarating," he said. "It's fun to watch Eric. When I first went to the games, just sitting there, I wasn't really comfortable being there. Everyone knows my past, knows how I am, and I felt sort of self-conscious. But Gary Weatherford and his wife helped. They showed me how to make it through there, not to worry about the things that I have done, but worry about the things that I'm trying to do. Gary and his wife were a godsend because if it wasn't for them Eric probably would have been in trouble now and probably wouldn't be going to school, wouldn't be educated or anything."

The Weatherfords attended all the home games, sitting close to the Anderson bench. Charles Bush watched from five rows up directly across the court from the bench. One night Anderson had little difficulty in running up a big score and Hecklinski removed Eric early in the fourth quarter. Charles stood up, put on his coat, and climbed down the bleachers. It was almost time for work. He stopped for a moment and looked across the court to the bench, catching Eric's eye. Charles put an imaginary phone to his ear. He would call. They would talk.

Bush, fifty-one, was a small man with long hair that hung in back below his neck. At the games he looked disheveled — sneakers with no laces, a worn coat. But he was dressed up coming from work. He had on a white shirt, creased trousers, polished brown shoes. His apartment furnishings were few — a sofa, two chairs, and a television set. But his new home was spotless and the sun shone in. "I work so hard to try to save, but every time I get a hundred dollars I have to pay some bill," he said. The television would have to go if he were pressed too hard, but he wanted the TV to help make the place feel like home when Eric or his other sons stopped by. Charles, twenty-one, who said he was "separated temporarily" from his wife, already had moved in. It gave Charles Sr. a feeling he hadn't known in years — that he was helping someone.

"When my wife passed away, I wound up getting in trouble," he said. "I got involved in drugs. Got in trouble with the law. I was involved with a lot of people from Detroit, Ohio, Michigan, and one weekend we all came back to Anderson. You know, I got caught at home with drugs. They came in. Kicked the door in. Arrested me."

When he was in jail he and Eric spoke on the phone.

"He told me that he understood," said Charles. "I didn't really know if he did or not, because I didn't even understand what I was doing. I was just doing it. But I guess the biggest thing out of all of it is that he really told me he loved me, he was sorry I had to be in jail, and that he'd always be there for me. And when I got out he told me the very same thing. It seemed like he had grown a foot taller by the time I saw him."

Eric had run the streets growing up and had continued to when his father went to jail. But when he was in eighth grade at Northside Middle School he met Cindy Weatherford, a teacher. He was in detention. She was in charge. While he was reluctant to talk much, she found him polite. And she learned enough to know he had numerous basic needs. She could see his basketball shoes had holes. She told Gary and Gary bought him new ones. Gary owned an auto repair service in Anderson, and over the years had provided odd jobs for Anderson High basketball players. They were struck both by Bush's poverty and a quiet, seemingly undemanding personality.

Gary recalled, "He had no structure in his life." Added Cindy, "He didn't have a coat."

Increasingly he visited their home and often would stay overnight. Gary would take him to school in the mornings. Some nights when he didn't stay over he wouldn't show up for school; Gary would go looking for him, pound on the door, and wake him up. "I'm sure he despised me for doing that," said Gary. A few months later when he was with them, Eric cut his finger and had to be taken to an emergency room. But the Weatherfords lacked a medical release so he could be treated. It was then they decided they needed legal guardianship.

At first Eric balked. He went to talk with his father. But his father persuaded him to take the Weatherfords up on their generosity. "His father realized that until he got his life in order he wasn't going to be able to help Eric out," said Cindy. "Eric took it as a rejection. We talked about that a great deal, the fact that it took a lot for his father to do that. I think it surprised Eric that his father told him he should try to understand why people were doing what they were doing for him."

That was August 1994. Eric was just beginning high school. The Weatherfords had a child, Bethany, in the same class at Anderson. "We love him as if he were our son," said Gary. It took until spring 1995 before Eric accepted them fully — and accepted the rules of the household. "I don't care if you're ever going to play basketball, you're going to school," Gary told Eric. But as a sophomore he got a D in English on his report card. It happened before the Marion game. "Guess what," Gary said to him. "You're not going to start." Eric said other players had D's. "But they don't live with us," Cindy told him.

"Let's think about this," a surprised Hecklinski responded to Gary Weatherford. The coach had never had parents asking him to bench one of his players — his star, at that. Marion was going to be a difficult game.

"Can you take something away from him at home?" Hecklinski asked Gary — to no avail. "Okay. Okay. If I have to put him in, can I put him in?" Hecklinski asked.

"We'd like him out at least a half," Gary responded.

Hecklinski waited until midway through the second quarter. Bush scored 27 points and Anderson won. And he worked harder in school. In the winter of his junior year he was sent home sick, but about noon of the second day he phoned Cindy, teaching by then at rival Anderson Highland High. "Can I go back to school? I can't miss any more classes." She had to wonder, Is this the Eric Bush who moved in with us?

By his junior year he had fully adjusted to the Weatherfords' role. "They're the best thing that ever happened to me," he said one day after practice. "They just picked me up. Without them I don't know where I would have been." But there still existed an undercurrent of neighborhood tension created by acquaintances of the Weatherfords who did not appreciate an integrated household.

The Weatherfords also had taken in Marquis Terrell, an Anderson senior basketball player, on a temporary basis. Terrell also is black. Acquaintances of the Weatherfords expressed skepticism, others suspicion. "They say, 'It won't work.' Some think we're up to something illegal, that we have these kids selling drugs," said Cindy. "It's awful. Others say, 'Well, they're basketball players, that's why we're doing it.' I don't know what we stand to get from them being players. These people don't get it. We don't want anything. It comes down to color. If everybody did not see color it'd be okay."

After Eric turned sixteen he asked for a car — he saw one he wanted, a white '85 Cadillac with more than 100,000 miles on it. "An old tank," Gary called it. He bought it for a thousand dollars. But as a friend had predicted, it wasn't long before Eric was stopped by police. Gary found out one day when Eric came home and said, "I hate white people." He would be stopped four times; four times he was told to proceed when all was found to be in order. Gary bought him a less conspicuous beige 1984 Buick Electra.

"It's difficult to be a black kid, not just in Anderson but anywhere," said Gary. "Eric got searched at the mall. The white kid he was with didn't. Then one day I took Eric and four of his friends down to Indianapolis. We went to this shoe store — I was going to buy them all shoes. It was going to be a pretty good sale. They wandered off to look at the shoes, and by the time I looked up the store people were watching the kids like they were going to take the shoes. I said, 'Let's go. I don't think we're wanted here.'

"You can see why that frustration sets in with Eric. And this whole experience has opened my eyes to the world out there."

Purdue coach Gene Keady, encountered a few weeks later watching a high school game in Indianapolis, said that Bush was a top college prospect. Purdue was scouting him regularly. Bush weighed only 165 pounds, but Keady didn't hesitate in saying that he would be strong enough to compete in the Big Ten. "Size doesn't matter," said Keady, "when you have that kind of speed."

Basketball held the promise of yet another dramatic change in Bush's life, since, even as a junior, he was being considered by big-name colleges. Hecklinski wanted the best for Bush and at times thought he would do well under Bob Knight. Weatherford wasn't so sure about that. Bush had experienced enough trauma.

"He's had a tough life," Hecklinski said. "I think the thing that affected him more than anything was his mother's death. She had the asthma attack, they rushed her to the hospital, and she was dead. It still has a big effect on him because he thinks a lot about his mother. He and his mother were really close. He told me his mother was just like him, smiled all the time. Everybody liked her.'' On her birthday and Mother's Day Eric would visit her grave. The first time he went to the cemetery he couldn't find the grave site, and got momentarily flustered. Tears came to his eyes.

"So it's been tough," said Hecklinski. "But maybe it's no tougher than any of these kids who come from the inner cities who have so little. He's got his guardians, who really care for him and try to make life a whole lot easier for him. I think there are times that he struggles with it. And I think there's times when his guardians try to discipline him and put some things on him where he tries to fight them. Every now and then we have to remind him, 'This is what's best for you, and in order for you to make it, this is the road you have to take.'"

Batesville's Michael Menser was a copy of Larry Bird not in size or potential but in a personality devoid of all pretension, in his love of the game, in the way he played it and the way he learned it, largely on his own in the solitude of an Indiana town.

Such a person still existed — the Hoosier of the imagination. He was the iconographic figure, up at sunrise, shooting baskets at sunset, his parents and older sister at hand — a living Rockwell family portrait. Here were the Mensers in a one-story stone house on Cedar Lane, Batesville, just a few miles from Bobby Plump's Pierceville farmhouse with its hoop nailed to a post. Menser had his hoop on a modern backyard court, but he'd never asked for anything special.

Young Menser was scarcely more talkative than Bird at age seventeen. Menser wasn't as shy as Bird, who in the beginning wasn't comfortable leaving French Lick. But Menser had no particular desire to go east to an Atlantic Coast Conference school or west to someplace glamorous like UCLA, or for that matter even the Big Ten. Not once had anyone heard him say, as so many Indiana kids do, how much he'd give to go to Bloomington. This alone set him apart.

"Growing up, I was always told I wasn't good enough to play college ball because I was from a small town, but I knew I could." That was Bird talking, although it could have been Menser. Bird possessed a quiet, genuine confidence, based on his basketball knowledge and know-how. Bird: "I taught myself things like a fadeaway shot because I knew I wouldn't be jumping over too many people. I just worked at it, that's all."

As a guard Menser had taught himself how to get free from bigger, faster opponents and how to keep up with them surprisingly well on defense. When Batesville played Anderson he faced the faster Eric Bush. But, a Bird-like compensator, Menser knew when to make his moves, and when he did he showed a fast first stride.

"I was impressed with how quick he is," Menser said of Bush. "He left me standing three or four times." Yet Menser outscored Bush, popping from outside or sliding past him gracefully amid the fury of a physical game.

Menser expressed the same philosophy as Bird. "You've got to know how to use your quickness because Bush is probably twice as quick as me. You've just got to pick your spots, and where to go. Dribble one way, cross over, and go back. You have to reverse pivot. Little things. I learned them playing AAU against some of the toughest guards in the nation."

He played against some of them in Las Vegas, where big-name coaches and scouts watched him. Bob Gibbons, who published the All-Star Sports scouting report, wrote: "Michael Menser is one of the top true point guard prospects in the country and the best point guard in the state of Indiana." Garry Donna of *Hoosier Basketball* magazine observed that Menser made his outstanding teammates on the Bloomington Red AAU team even better, "the ultimate sign of an elite team player."

Still, hardly any college phoned Batesville. "They thought he was too small," said his coach, Melvin Siefert. "Indiana State got a steal. They must be laughing."

Sitting in the stands game after game watching him prompted wonder. Menser is small, very small, but, still, how could *all* the big colleges pass on him?

It was as if Menser's numbers had been fed into some sophisticated machinery and a red light flashed. Maybe it was the number 145, his weight. A little less after practices, a little more after one of Jenny Menser's meals. But surely his weight would have increased after a year or so at one of the high-powered institutions where athletes' bodies are molded with an attentiveness often not given to their minds. "I'd say it was his height — if he were six two the colleges would want him because they would put the weight on him," said Jerry Craig, the coach of Rushville, after losing by fifteen points to Batesville.

"Some people are caught up on physical limits," said Duke University's coach Mike Krzyzewski. "If you're not six two, you're eliminated. If you don't have a certain amount of speed, you're eliminated. Instead of looking at the whole package and seeing if that package can win. We don't put physical limitations on." As a result Duke has had its share of small but proficient guards. "The one common thread is that they really know how to win. They're competitive. Their teams in high school usually won and they were the main reason."

But Krzyzewski said he had never heard of Menser. "I'm really not familiar with the young man. One of my assistants may be." He elaborated on a head coach's busy schedule that might prevent him from knowing about every possible recruit. "People can miss on somebody. Those are the kinds of players who win in the first round and second round of the NCAAs." The other thing, Krzyzewski said, was, what had Menser done last summer? Getting seen by scouts at a major camp was important, and more: "In that short period, was he able to perform up to his usual caliber?"

Menser had not been invited to the Nike camp in Indianapolis in the summer of 1996. It featured supposedly the most talented junior, sophomore, and freshman high school players in the country — mostly juniors. "We tried," said Siefert. "We couldn't get any kind of response." Anderson's Hecklinski and other Indiana high school coaches said that Menser had deserved the chance to demonstrate his ability to the college coaches who flock to the Nike camp.

Butler offered Menser a scholarship. Illinois State offered a scholarship to him but offered the same one to another prospect — it would go to whoever took it first. Menser hesitated, and it was gone. But he wasn't feeling sorry for himself in the least when he went to Terre Haute for his official visit to Indiana State in the fall of 1996. Siefert had told him, "If you like it, great; if you don't, we'll sit back and see what happens."

Michael liked Indiana State. "My sister's there," he said. "It's not too far from my family. They can watch me play. I met the players, I liked them. I liked the coach. I was happy. I decided it was the place for me."

That was the extent of Menser's recruiting experience. He went back to shooting baskets in the Batesville gym and at the hoop behind his house, across a field from a cemetery.

"I'd hate to know the number of hours he's logged on a basketball court," said Bryan Helvie, who coached Menser in eighth grade when he was five feet four, ninety pounds. Helvie smiled as he thought back four years. "He could play the game even then. He could shoot from long range. He could penetrate. The most impressive thing about him was the way he could handle the ball. Nobody could take it from him."

He kept getting better — if only marginally bigger. "I think I weighed ninety-nine when I was a freshman," said Menser. "I put down 106. I gave myself some weight. Everybody was asking me what grade I was in — why we had an elementary kid on the team." He could hear people talking during warm-ups: "How old are you? Are you in high school?"

What he wanted to be was six feet. His father was five nine, his mother much shorter. Little marks on his wall at home told of Michael's incremental gains. At midseason of his senior year he reached five eleven and a half in his bare feet. "I still think I'm going up because my knees hurt once in a while and I don't shave that often," he said.

And: "I have really big feet."

Pause: "Maybe I'm a late bloomer — six five."

The last, of course, was a joke. Menser didn't joke much. Most of the time he was happily impassive. One day, he whistled while he did an odd job in the receptionist's office at the high school. He almost never gave in to an emotional outburst during games. He played almost dreamily, until he'd spring forward to the basket or shoot a jump shot. He did two things well: he could handle the ball flawlessly with either hand at high speed, and he could shoot. It's rare for a guard to be able to do both at such a level of excellence, and at the same time be able to shift from one to the other, from penetrating with the ball to jump-shooting in a blink.

He steered through the traffic of taller opponents with his deft dribbling — remarkably well given that his hands are small. But he has long arms. Bob Cousy had long arms. Menser's droop almost to his knees. Those mantis arms helped him steal the ball from taller opponents after they'd rebounded; he was a master at dribbling out of a pack of players, having entered the forest of bodies empty-handed.

Against rival Greensburg an opponent went up for a rebound. Menser, behind him, knew he couldn't get the ball himself but he leaped high enough to reach over the player's shoulder and tap it to a teammate. "He does the little things," said Helvie. Like Bird. When opponents jumped out to the perimeter on him, fearful that he'd hit a three-pointer, Menser would find a teammate underneath the basket for a layup. When something like that happened, Batesville fans would roar. If not every college coach knew of him, he nevertheless gained an increasing following around the state as he kept leading the Bulldogs to victories.

"Pressure?" exclaimed Rushville's Jerry Craig. "His attitude is, 'Give me the ball. I'm going to win the game at the end.' Defense, too. He'll take on someone at the end of a game."

"One thing that's helped make him successful," said Siefert, "is that he doesn't worry about things he can't control."

Menser had the attitude of a pro — a confident, controlled pro — like Bird and the players he dreamed about. "Until I was about ten," he said, "I was going to be this awesome running back for the Chicago Bears. I was going to be Walter Payton. But then I started playing basketball."

Did he see himself as the next John Stockton?

"I like Kevin Johnson's game more. Kevin Johnson's my favorite point guard. He's a shooter. And he's streaky. Stockton doesn't shoot that much. But Johnson, I love his move where he goes between his legs and takes one dribble and then puts something like a finger roll on it." Menser's bedroom walls were covered with photos and posters of Kevin Johnson and Michael Jordan.

Batesville was an ideal place to dream about the game and its idols, and even a possible high school state championship. Batesville had done well in Siefert's first three years, which were Menser's first three years. When Menser was a freshman and sixth man, Batesville made the final sixteen before losing to Ben Davis. Batesville lost in the 1995 regionals, by two points, and in the 1996 regionals by one. "Last year was hard, especially for the seniors," said Menser. After the last game he tried to cheer them: "'Keep your heads up, guys. You just got beat by the eleventh team in the state by one point. It was a hell of a game.'. . .

"This year I'm going to do everything I can to prevent that from happening again. I think it's possible basically because we've played the competition, we've been up against Anderson, and we're not going into the tournament thinking, 'Oh, gosh, this is going to be a big school, they have a thousand more kids than us, they must be awesome or something.' I think with the team we have we can play with anybody.

"I'm against the four classes. I like the one class because it's Hoosier Hysteria. I don't like the idea that you're a state champion but there are three other teams that are state champions. If we were state champions, I'd want us to be the only state champions. I think we can be. We can be the last team to win the state tourney, one class. You look down the road and you see Milan and you say it's possible. Basketball is so weird. Anything can happen."

And if they were to win the championship?

"Nothing's going to change," he said. "I'm going to lifeguard this summer and cut grass with my cousin."

A Christmas card in one of Marti Recker's scrapbooks told, in effect, how long a coach had been dreaming the dream of a state championship. The card was a color photograph of Luke Recker's first DeKalb High team posed on the steps of the Indianapolis Dome in November 1993 and it said: "Luke, we will go to the Dome someday! Coach Hawkins."

It was now or never.

It was January and beginning to look like never.

Two weeks after DeKalb had lost its two games in the Hall of Fame Classic it was beaten on its home floor by East Noble. East Noble, DeKalb, and Fort Wayne South Side, with the six-eight, Purdue-bound Cameron Stephens, were the top teams in northeastern Indiana — the ones with the best chance to make it through the Fort Wayne semistate to the final four in Indianapolis. East Noble also had beaten Fort Wayne South Side in Fort Wayne. Ten days after its victory at DeKalb, East Noble had to return there for the Northeast Hoosier Conference tournament. Inevitably East Noble and DeKalb would meet in that tournament's championship game. The Associated Press weekly poll rated East Noble fifteenth and DeKalb twentieth; the coaches, on the basis of DeKalb's Hall of Fame losses, had dropped DeKalb out of their top twenty. The rematch had to be rescheduled from a Saturday night to a Monday night because of high winds and drifting snow. Northeastern Indiana looked like a Currier and Ives winter-wonderland print, but it felt like the inside of a freezer. By Monday night the DeKalb gym was jammed to capacity with people infected by both basketball fever and cabin fever.

East Noble was a prototypical Indiana team. It had a respected coach in Marty Johnson, a tall man who kept his tie loosened during games. He taught a patient, controlled offense. In its first game with DeKalb, East Noble's defense collapsed on Recker and held him to ten points. In that game Recker got two quick fouls, turning him conservative and adding to East Noble's confidence. Since then, the pressure had been on Hawkins to find a way to get something from the rest of the team while persuading Recker to be more selective with his shots after his display of gunnery in the two Hall of Fame games. If DeKalb couldn't win the second time around against East Noble, it would be a team falling embarrassingly short of its aspirations.

It had come down to this: DeKalb's players were on the verge of losing their confidence and fan interest. If DeKalb's season fell apart, Recker might well lose the "Mr. Basketball" honor. That would be a drastic turn of events for the player hailed as the second coming of Rex Chapman, he of the forty-four-inch vertical leap. In a sport that had come to be predominantly black at the pro and top-college levels, Recker was unusual: a potential marquee white talent.

He was one of the most gifted white players since Chapman came along fifteen years earlier in neighboring Kentucky. And Recker was sturdier than Chapman, whose pro career had been interrupted repeatedly by injuries. Recker had been experiencing a state-wide adulation, as Chapman had at the same age. Recker's photo adorned magazine covers, his name kept coming up on television and radio sports programs. But after he'd taken those sixty-one shots in the Hall of Fame Classic, Recker faced a backlash of criticism.

People battled to get on the Internet to say that Cameron Stephens and Jamaal Davis were the better players, that Recker was overrated, that he was not a team player, that he was a bad example because he had kicked the chair after the first Hall of Fame loss. This was not idle cyberspace chat, it was star wars, Indiana-style, and Recker was the target.

A surprise source intervened.

"As I read the postings in this forum," Batesville's coach Siefert wrote one morning on his laptop, "I am concerned that the debate about one player over another, one team over another is becoming very negative. Let us keep in mind that we are talking about 16, 17 & 18 year old kids. They play the game for the love of the game, not for people to criticize their every move. Luke has taken enough abuse, allow him, and the others to enjoy their senior year. A fun debate is great but let's try to keep it positive!"

Siefert was ahead of many coaches with knowledge of the Internet. During the day at school he carried his computer in a book bag, and when he had time perused such Internet offerings as "Indiana's Game" — devoted strictly to high school basketball — and "High School Forum."

From his Batesville office Siefert calmed the masses. Messages proliferated under such headlines as: "Good Call, Coach"; "Melvin Is Right"; "Thank you, Coach"; and "My Deepest Apology."

A Webbed world as well as a full gym awaited the second DeKalb–East Noble game. Hawkins combed his hair in front of the bathroom mirror of his office. "This is going to be a great game tonight," he said, turning from the mirror, ready. "We're going to win tonight. This is truly what it's all about."

He believed the players in the next room were so ready that he didn't have to say much before they would burst forth for the rematch. He walked in, stood in their midst, waited a moment until all were quiet and still, and said just this: "Very few teams get a second chance. Let's do it."

They did, 53–41. Recker scored 23 points and had six steals and five rebounds. His play was erratic early — he missed seven straight shots. But he settled down and DeKalb's team played well, especially in the way it smothered East Noble with a pressing zone defense. Afterward, Hawkins praised his players for their defense — praised them effusively. He repeated himself, genuinely pleased and at the same time making sure to erase any remaining doubts created by three losses. "Man," he told them, "that was something out there tonight. If that doesn't make you feel unbelievable then there is something wrong with you. If you stop to think about how everybody contributed, from a big play offensively to a great play defensively, from a big rebound to a great steal, man, it was incredible. It was incredible. I don't think I've ever seen thirty-two sustained minutes of defensive play like that. You guys should be proud of yourselves. . . .

"I tell you what. You take away the Hall of Fame, this team has matched everything last year's team has done. I'm so sick of hearing that. We matched it all. I've said all along, this team has the potential to be better at the end than last year's team because of one reason, defense. Because defense wins championships. Tonight that effort was unbelievable. You guys were champions."

In his office later Hawkins expressed regret that he'd overemphasized the game with Anderson in the Hall of Fame. But he said: "That Hall of Fame experience has let this team come together, let Luke see how he has to incorporate his teammates into what we're trying to get done in terms of offensive play." DeKalb's record was 12–3, a crisis seemed averted, and: "We're going to hone everything down and be ready for the tournament. I think we'll be peaking at the right time." Hawkins, the relentless one, would be in his office at 5 A.M. preparing for Columbia City.

Recker also felt better after the victory over East Noble. "I wish I could take a few things back from the Hall of Fame Classic, especially the Anderson loss," he said. "What was so tough about the Anderson loss was after. I remember being in the hotel room and talking to Luke Barnett and saying, 'Man, we got to play in four hours.' We were saying, 'We've got to go out and play hard,' but the loss ate up the whole team. Most high school kids in hotel rooms, they can get a little crazy; but I remember after that first game everybody just went back to their rooms and sat there. We sat there and talked and we couldn't get over the loss.

"Then East Noble got our spirits down. I kind of sat back and said to myself, this isn't supposed to be happening. I didn't sleep after the East Noble game. I couldn't get myself to sleep, I was so disappointed. But our team got together and we said we're going to have to do this together. The end of the year is what really matters and we think that we can be one of the top teams in the state, and have a shot at winning the state. The last three games have been a lot of fun. People have been saying, 'You're not scoring thirty points, what's the matter?' I say, 'It doesn't matter. We're having fun and we're playing team ball.'"

Hawkins had assured Recker that he wasn't going to stop him from shooting altogether, turn off his point source like a spigot. Hawkins said: "Those of us with the great players have a chance to go a long way because they can do things other players can't. No matter how much they double on Luke, I still have to find a way to get the ball in his hands for shots."

Recker's responsibilities at home increased. His parents' divorce was finalized in January. His father said: "It's unfortunate he's in that situation. It's unfortunate he has to assume a bit more responsibility. But . . . we always stressed to the children to watch out for one another. He's done a fine job of adjusting to the situation, as all the kids have." And, he added, Luke was "smart enough to know how his dad makes his money."

Clair Recker had been promoted in 1995 to general manager of the McCleery-Cumming Company, which manufactured calendars for advertising. It was located in Washington, Iowa, four hundred miles away. He still had managed to drive home for most of Luke's games his junior year, but the number slipped to about half the games his senior year. "I know the distance didn't get any longer," he said, "but the trip seems longer." Typically he would take a half day's vacation on Fridays and drive back to Iowa on Sundays.

The father had grown up, one of twelve children, in northwestern Ohio. After playing college basketball for Bluffton, he played in industrial leagues. He used to take Luke — Lucas was his given name — and his sisters along, and that's how they were introduced to the game. "Luke spent a lot of time out on the floor. He always dribbled in the house. Even sitting at the fireplace he always had a basketball in his hands, like it was an extension of his body. One of the first things we did when we moved to Indiana was put a nice court in the backyard. It's an official one-third court. I wanted him to have this court with the right dimensions. I made it legitimate size.

"I knew very early that he was going to be an exceptional player, when he was only four or five years of age. We put up posts in the basement and he'd do figure eights around them, dribble both left- and right-handed." Clair coached an AAU team Luke played on as a grade-schooler. "But I thought he might be a baseball player. If he was to make money at it, I thought baseball would be a sport more accommodating to him. But after eighth grade he quit baseball. He wanted to devote all his time to basketball because he wanted to play varsity as a freshman. I told him that was a pretty lofty goal."

A DeKalb senior named Nate Tatman smoothed an opening for Recker in the seventh game of his freshman season. Hawkins had called Tatman to his office. "'I need to talk to you about something,'" Hawkins recalled. "I was feeling so uncomfortable with what I was going to do. But Nate went right with it. He looked across the table and said, 'I know what you want to say. Luke should be starting.' I told him, 'You're going to be the best sixth man anybody's ever seen.' And he would come in and lead the press. A team player in the true sense."

All Recker wanted was to start as a freshman. And he did. But he never anticipated celebrity and its burden. "I still look at myself as a kid, and I do things I wish I could take back," he said. "For instance, the Hall of Fame, my emotions at the end of the game. I was just so upset I just kicked a chair. And people saw it and pretty soon a lot of people got on the Internet and they're writing about how much of an attitude problem I am and stuff. It gets to me a little bit. I sit there and say, you know, these people don't know me and they're writing bad stuff about me, saying my attitude's awful. I try not to think about it, but it's tough.

"I try to do everything I can to be a good person. But I'm in the public eye, and it seems anything I do, everybody finds out about it, it's published, and that's the toughest thing. I'll be saying something to one of my friends and someone will overhear it, and like that, everybody knows it. That's the toughest part about it. Really, everything I do I've got to be thinking."

He couldn't have imagined a downside to the game when he was younger. He had the court in his backyard with a glass backboard and the freedom to put up hundreds of shots a day. He got so good he traveled the country, and now he played like someone years older. But he was only seventeen and facing the realization that his childhood had ended, and probably had some time ago. His parents had never pushed or prodded, it's just that the game yanked him early into the future. "I try to be a kid," he said, "but really I can't be a little kid."

From the look of him, making his unhurried way from class to basketball practice, Merrillville's Jamaal Davis didn't appear to have a care. He was dressed crisply in a multicolored long-sleeved shirt and creased khakis. He talked easily, articulately. He smiled often. He said that someday he might like to be a television commentator;

you could envision him someday in the expert analyst's chair on ESPN. Sometimes during conversations, he gave the impression, with his gestures and facial expressions, that he was polishing a certain cadenced delivery to use while giving interviews as the collegiate and professional athlete he imagined he would be, or in the far future as a TV commentator.

An articulate fellow, a visitor told his coach, Jim East.

"Jamaal can charm you," said East.

East's remark seemed more good-natured than a warning. East and the six-eight Davis seemed to have gotten past a taut relationship, which had culminated the previous season in a shouting match and a two-game suspension for Davis after the coach had removed him from a jamboree game to give others a chance to play. Most of their disagreements this season pertained to basketball tactics. Such as: "Jamaal, why didn't you take that shot? You were open." And Jamaal, musing after looking at the tape: "Yeah, I was open. Why didn't I?"

Davis was an unusual young player in that most often he looked to pass before shooting. As a senior he professed an increased responsibility to involve the other players so he passed off even more, and his statistics verified that. His scoring was slightly down, but his assists were up. His rebounds and blocked shots also were up. East had gone into the season pleading with him to score more, and Davis hit a season-high 30 points in a victory at Gary Roosevelt. Ironically, Merrillville was doing better than East had hoped with Davis helping spread the scoring among his teammates.

But could East expect another outburst from Jamaal as in his junior year? Could East expect a smooth ride from his team in general?

On the first question he wasn't sure. As for the second he knew better. Not with this team, he said. There was always something; often minor, but something disconcerting, something to take away from his desire simply to teach the game and, not incidentally, win. Here was something occupying the mind of his star player:

What of this matter of possible marriage that Davis brought up out of the blue to a visitor? Davis said he wanted to marry a sixteen-year-old Merrillville freshman who had a daughter almost two years old.

East clapped his forehead. It wasn't the first time he'd heard that. "Jamaal's a good kid. He's a bit of a dreamer," said East. "I think he sees himself as the savior of this girl."

Davis referred to the young woman as his "fiancée" and talked dreamily of a June wedding. He said he wanted to take her with him to Purdue, which had signed him, and there in the college neighborhood she could go on with her high school education. He was playing basketball, studying, seeing his girlfriend, and preparing for college-entrance exams — the SAT and ACT. But he expressed confidence that he could handle everything. Davis said he would score high enough on the tests to be academically eligible to play as a freshman at Purdue, and that he had the high school grades he needed as well.

East, seated in his office, lowered his head. He wished that were true but said that he believed it would take Davis at least another year to become eligible to play at Purdue. East said that Davis did not have the requisite grade-point average in his core courses at Merrillville even before taking the SAT or ACT. East implied that it would require an academic miracle for Davis to play at Purdue as a freshman — and East was too practical a person to expect a miracle.

Not only was Davis trying to keep his grades up and be the team leader that East wanted, he was trying to be a guiding light to his younger brother, John, who by his mother's account had been approaching schoolwork desultorily and basketball almost wordlessly — so that East didn't know what was on the younger Davis's mind.

John frustrated East because he wanted the sophomore to "step up" and be his small forward — an area of agreement between East and Jamaal. When John became academically ineligible at midseason, he already had "stepped up" enough to be sixth man and showed promise of being a starter. The team's seventh man also was ruled academically ineligible, leaving East dismayed. A player was suspended one game after arguing with a teacher. East called this "the most frustrating season in my seventeen years at Merrillville." He began thinking that the closest he would get to the final four in Indianapolis was a seat in the stands.

Jamaal professed disappointment with his brother. "At my press conference I really gave him a lot of hype," he said, referring to the day he signed with Purdue. "I told him how he not only let himself down but he let me down. And for him to let me down, I think that affected him."

"Now Jamaal feels like I guess everything's on his shoulders for this year," said his mother, Belinda Brown, who operated "Brown's Professional Services: A Business Resource Center," in Gary.

Basketball-related problems paled compared with the life experiences Jamaal had related — the pervasiveness of drug dealing on the streets of Gary that he'd managed to avoid, the proliferation of roving gangs that he said he'd never belonged to (although he claimed to know gang members), the shooting of his friend with the flashy car, and the holdup of his mother, stepmother, and brother. Belinda Brown said that Jamaal's father had interested their son in basketball at the age of seven and that strong family support had always helped Jamaal. Even though she and his father were divorced and remarried, all parties "respected" one another and watched out for the children. It was in Jamaal's interest to move to Merrillville with his father, although he often visited his mother in Gary before she moved. It was heart-wrenching to see the ruins of downtown Gary, with so many businesses closed and boarded up, buildings burned or gone. If ever there was a boulevard of broken dreams it was Broadway, in Gary.

In an article titled "Gangland," on February 21, 1997, Gary's Post-Tribune reported that Chicago-based gangs had threatened the life of Gary mayor Scott King in the fall of 1996 because he refused to open city-owned park buildings to them for a so-called peace summit. Early in 1997, Sheriff John Buncich of Lake County, which includes Gary and Merrillville, revealed similar threats against him and other top county police officers; gangs were angry because a crackdown by Buncich's department on gang activity was hurting drug sales.

Of 107 homicides in Gary in 1996, the Post-Tribune reported, 46 involved black males younger than 25 and nearly all of them were drug or gang related. Of almost 100 gangs in northwestern Indiana, the paper said, 46 were based in Gary.

"If you were raised in a place and people knew you, they didn't mess with you unless you were involved in what they were doing," said Belinda Brown. "Jamaal and John had never been involved in what those people were doing. It was, 'Hey, man, how ya doin'?,' and then if the others went off to rob something, steal a car, whatever, that's what they do. You don't have to do what another person does. We just don't allow the boys to run the streets. Both my boys have pagers. I want to know where they are. They've never done any loose running around.

"Most of the things that happen in the city of Gary happen . . . if you're involved with drugs, buying or selling. If you are a gang member, they'll usually retaliate against each other, one gang area against another gang area in the sale or purchase of drugs. Now if you're not involved in that, the likelihood of surviving in the city is much better."

John's experience in trying to make grades in the more demanding Merrillville High after Gary was similar to Jamaal's, and his mother hoped that he would learn that basketball had its benefits and that he would study harder to stay eligible.

East monitored Jamaal's academics and as much of his life as he could in Jamaal's first two years at Merrillville. But that approach angered Belinda Brown. Proud of the family's efforts in raising Jamaal, she was upset with the coach on the eve of the state championship game in 1995 because of an article in the *Post-Tribune*. She didn't like a sports feature story, although she had it taped to a wall in her office with some other newspaper articles about Jamaal, because she believed it gave too much credit to East and his wife and daughter, both teachers, for Jamaal's academic improvement. "I thank them, to this day, for helping me develop good study habits," Jamaal was quoted as saying of the East family.

"He acted as if this kid came from the ghetto somewhere and he rescued him," she said irately of East.

East winced at the recollection. He considered the article well-intentioned, but he determined to stay out of Jamaal's personal life as much as he could. But to East, as to most coaches, anything off-court that might distract a player from basketball was something to be dealt with. East had been spoiled by three dominant seniors who provided the leadership for the 1995 team. The current team relied solely on Jamaal for leadership, and with his 1995 team fresh in mind, East wished he had one or two more leaders. Still, at times, Davis sounded like East's echo.

"Our team's still mentally young," he said. "Our team doesn't have that fire, that desire to win like the '95 team, I don't feel. That team would dive on the floors. This team's a more cool team, more finesse. Our recoveries — getting loose balls — are way down from two years ago. This kind of frustrates me a little.

"Two years ago other teams couldn't focus on one guy, they had to focus on three. This year they can focus on me if the rest of the guys aren't playing well. This year we have six seniors and I'd say four of them don't say much. The younger guys don't know what it takes to win. The guards are more tentative than they should be. And that's frustrating to me."

East hadn't wanted to play a three-guard offense, but in 1996–97 he had no choice. He'd always been a coach with a preference for big inside players who would power up to the basket. In 1986 East came across Dikembe Mutombo in Lubumbashi, Zaire, during a trip to Africa with three other Indiana high school coaches to conduct clinics for a U.S. Information Agency program. Mutombo went on to play at Georgetown and in the NBA, but as raw a talent as he was in Zaire, East recognized him as a prospect and wanted to get information on him to some college coach; a cultural affairs officer for the U.S. embassy in Kinshasa contacted Georgetown. While East had never coached anyone who had developed into a Mutombo, he had a reputation for coaching big players well, and in Jamaal had his best big man ever.

On a January Friday night at home against Crown Point, East's three-guard offense excelled. His left-handed point man, a sophomore named Eugene Wilson, scored 20 points, including important second-half baskets that helped Merrillville rally to a thirteenth-straight victory. Davis provided the margin of victory, 62–61, on a put-back, a falling-away seven-footer, with 3.5 seconds remaining. In the final four and a half minutes Jamaal collected six of Merrillville's last seven points. He also grabbed four rebounds and blocked a shot. He finished with 26 points, 15 rebounds, and five blocks. He could be brilliant.

"We probably shouldn't have won," said East. But he couldn't imagine a better ending to a hard-fought game than Davis's buzzer beater. At last the coach was "feeling it," the possibility that maybe Merrillville could make it to the final four playing three guards and having few reserves. Merrillville was undermanned, but Jamaal, having experienced the '95 title game, was aiming for a second opportunity in Indianapolis.

Still, some things about Jamaal troubled East. He'd weighed about 215 or 220 as a junior, but less as a senior — he had not put on muscle with a weight program, nor had he been eating a proper diet, in East's opinion. The coach also worried that Davis lacked a clear view of his immediate future. East said that Davis wouldn't "deal with reality" and face up to his academic difficulties.

East was a demanding coach. His colleagues rated him an excellent bench coach. And he was demonstrating resourcefulness, playing three guards and winning. Clearly he wanted the best out of Davis during the season. East said that he had "dealt with Jamaal for a long time," liked him, and wanted him to do well after his graduation, too. But he was filled with doubts about Davis. Possibly Jamaal was filled with self-doubt; East wasn't sure after all those seasons as his coach. "Jamaal," said East, "is a mystery to me."

Huggy Dye, the "move-in" at North Central, in Indianapolis, liked to talk to his opponents. He smiled at them. He loved going one-on-one, and occasionally teammates would clear out for him. At six feet two, 185 pounds, he could change speeds suddenly; one moment he would be strolling with the ball, the next his long legs would be eating up the court in a blur as he lowered his shoulder and muscled for the basket. He liked to put his free hand on his opponent to keep him at a distance, an effective maneuver because of his long arms. He played defense with similar verve and occasional rule bending, hiking up his trunks and crouching in front of an opponent with the ball, sometimes mugging, sometimes pushing the opponent after that player had passed the ball and most people were following the flight of the ball. He played a game of intimidation.

Possibly the most influential person in Huggy Dye's life was a woman he met when he was in fifth grade in Danville, Illinois. Her name was Debby Chew. She was an elementary school teacher, but it was not in the classroom that she got his attention. She coached basketball, and while eleven-year-old Huggy already was certain he was headed for a career as a professional football player, he heeded Chew's call to basketball practice. At the first practice, neither he nor his classmates took Chew seriously. "Everybody was like, 'You're a lady, you don't know what you're talking about.'"

Then she demonstrated.

"Everybody went, 'Daaaang.'"

Debby Chew could dominate men's games and she developed

Huggy's game, beginning with the layup. "She's got a jump shot," said Huggy, clearing sleep from his eyes as he sat on a living-room sofa in his mother's apartment, wearing only dark blue basketball trunks. "Like one of my favorite moves is a reverse; she's got the best reverse I ever saw."

She changed the course of his life, or at least from one sport to another. "I told her, 'When I go to the NBA I'm going to look out for you,'" said Huggy.

Huggy smiled. He always could win you over. His aunt Mary Bryant took one look at him moments after he was born and nick-named him "Huggy Bear." She helped raise him, she loved him so much. As he grew older everyone in the family dropped the "Bear" and he became "Huggy." By eighth grade he had all his moves. By junior year at Danville High he was the full-grown Huggy and had a sizable reputation for playing a unique brand of full-court jazz. He had the game to go with the name.

But also that year Huggy had been in some mood his mother, Penny, found unexplainable, although she said that her breakup with Huggy's father may have been a factor. Huggy missed nine games his junior season — he was academically ineligible for seven after a long, lackadaisical spell, and out of action for two more when Penny benched him while trying to get him over a spell of moodiness and back to a happy Huggy.

Finally, she decided to move to Indianapolis. An administrative assistant at the pharmaceutical company Eli Lilly, she had been commuting from Danville to the Lilly office in the western Indiana town of Clinton. Tired of that, she applied for a transfer to Lilly's corporate headquarters in Indianapolis and began looking in the city for a school for Huggy. The son she would bring in tow to Indy was like no player ever to come down I-74. Her impending move found its way into the Danville press. When basketball coaches at a few Indianapolis schools heard that this marvelous, at-large talent was heading toward them, they took the news as if they'd heard the clacking of Samuel Morse's first message.

Not so at Ben Davis, which coincidentally was the school Huggy wanted to attend. He had heard of Ben Davis because of its basketball success and liked the idea of possibly playing in a title game. Penny Dye made an appointment with Steve Witty. Accounts from both individuals suggested their meeting never reached any sort of comfort level.

"It's a very awkward situation when people approach you about transferring to your school," Witty said later. "There are IHSAA rules against illegal recruiting." He said that he did not want to be put in the position of appearing to be doing anything wrong, and wished Penny Dye had done what Courtney James's mother had done two years before: enroll her son at the school, then come see him.

James was huge — six eight, 250 pounds at the time — and a huge talent. "For two years he played at Pike and both years he got kicked off the team," said Witty. "For two years I heard he was going to transfer to Ben Davis. Finally, he enrolled for the last nine weeks of his junior year. I didn't talk to him for seven weeks, although nobody would believe that. Finally I sat down with him and I said, 'Three things are going to have to happen before you can play for Ben Davis. You've accomplished one — in the classroom. Secondly, the IHSAA is going to have to approve your transfer. Thirdly, are you going to be willing to fulfill the expectations of our basketball program?'"

James and Damon Frierson led Ben Davis to its first state championship. At 32–1 it was one of the best teams in the history of Indiana basketball. The 1996 Ben Davis team wasn't nearly as good, but Witty's coaching carried a second straight title. When the Dyes arrived for a meeting, Witty assembled several school officials in part so that it would be clear he did not violate any recruiting rules. Having made the appointment well before, Penny Dye was upset that she had to wait while everyone gathered.

"That was a horrible visit," she said. "I'm talking to him and probably about twenty other people were in the same room, butting in on our conversation. All he told me was the three, four years of championships he had under his belt and he aimed to keep it that way. And he had all of his people returning and he was not changing it. I showed him all the newspaper clippings and articles of Huggy being invited to the Nike camp and he looked at them and said, 'That's good,' and just threw them on the table. It was just a horrible interview. It really was.

"I told Huggy, 'Read between the lines. He's more or less told us he's not changing his strategy for you or nobody else.' And I said, 'I'm not going to let you go to a school where you're just going to sit on the bench.' I said, 'I think your expertise is too good in basketball for you to just sit on the bench in your last year.' I felt really bad about taking him out of Danville over here anyway. I wasn't just going to place him anywhere."

She and Huggy went home to Danville, where she pondered their next move. North Central came to mind because a friend lived near the school and enjoyed the area. Like Witty and other Indianapolis coaches, North Central's Doug Mitchell knew about Dye. He knew that Huggy might be all he needed to make a run for the state championship. North Central was a school with a lackluster basketball history. Even Marvin Wood, of Milan fame, bowed out after nine seasons in the fifties and sixties with a 92–104 record. But Mitchell's fourth team promised to be special largely because of sophomore Jason Gardner. If Mitchell had but one more outstanding player . . . Penny Dye called and made an appointment.

There were few secrets among Indiana basketball coaches, and the word on Huggy was out, at least around Indianapolis, as coaches checked their Illinois sources. His sense of where he was on the court was always in the middle of the action, not all bad, but his transcript suggested he had been on the fringe of academic ambition. A good coach could always add another pearl to an impressive strand, but whether he could get him to peek inside a textbook was less certain.

"If you come here and you do what's asked of you — work

hard in the classroom — I'll give everything as a coach and a person back to you," Mitchell said he told Dye. "If you misbehave, I'll cut you. Life's too short. You begin to act like a fool, we will kick you off." The fact that Mitchell knew Dye had been academically ineligible for a time during the previous season impressed Penny Dye. "Mitchell," she said, "apparently did his homework."

She liked him. "He showed me around the building. He talked to me. He talked to Huggy. He said, 'I could take you out on the streets right now and show you probably a hundred of you.' He said, 'But the most important thing is your academics, your education.' He said, 'I don't care if you ever play ball. I'm concerned about your education. You may not like me sometimes if you choose to go to North Central because I'm going to stay on you. And there's going to come a time when you're just going to want to quit, probably want to cuss me out. But I'm going to be your father while you're here at this school.'

"Mitchell not once told Huggy he needed him. He told Huggy, 'I don't need you if you're going to come in here like you did in Danville.' When I left there I told Huggy, 'This is the school that, personally, I would choose.' Huggy still had his mind made up to go to Ben Davis because he thought the coach would change his mind.

"I said, 'You're not going to play there. He doesn't want you, Huggy. He does not want you.' I told him, 'You're going to North Central whether you like it or not.' And I started making preparations to start his summer school there and looking for a place to live."

One day Huggy was dribbling his basketball outside their new apartment in Indianapolis. He stopped and, as if finally realizing that North Central was going to be his school, said to her, "I'm going to be Coach Witty's worst nightmare."

"He was afraid that by coming here he wasn't going to be the man," explained Darrel Johnson, Penny Dye's fiancé. "Bigger schools, better talent. To move to a strange place, make new friends. A new coach. He didn't know whether he was going to fit into the system.

"He's a showboat," Johnson said. "His style is part showboat, part athleticism, part hard-nosed. You will notice him. You'll definitely notice him in some way, shape, or form."

"Even though Huggy's dad and I had been separated for a while, we were actually finalizing the divorce about the time he wasn't applying himself," said Penny Dye. "And Huggy was close to his dad. And [Huggy] was going through a lot of personal things and I think he just didn't care."

Clinton Dye and Clinton Jr. — that was Huggy — used to be like brothers, Huggy said. He didn't have a brother — his sister, Tia, was six years older — and he and his father would play basketball together. Huggy, though a grade-schooler, played in rugged outdoor games with the men; his father, when he got to choose a side, picked his son first. Huggy had a scar on his right eyelid "from an elbow, trying to play with the big boys."

The father "had a jump shot and a spin move," and he was "pretty strong, a talker." Now Huggy talked on the court. And he laughed on the court. "It's all in the game," he said.

Did opponents talk back?

"I get some of 'em to talk back. I guess they talk because I'm a talker. I don't know why they do it because it makes me even stronger. It just throws them off, and I just laugh at 'em. And afterwards, I just say, 'Nice game,' and go home."

But shortly after the move, Huggy's moodiness bubbled up as it had in Danville. Literally, he talked to himself.

"There were times I was so angry I'd just kick my basketball so hard, I'd just kick it as hard as I can," he said. "When I was in Danville I was being recruited by colleges, and I wondered if coming here would affect me playing at the next level. Whether it would make a difference between Division I or Division II. Or, would I get any playing time at all? Or, would I still be the Huggy Dye I know I am?

"My mom used to wake me up about four-something in the morning" — her transfer to Eli Lilly in Indianapolis hadn't yet come through so she still was commuting to Clinton, only from the other direction. She would drop him off at North Central. "I'd go to the gym about five-something in the morning, and shoot. 'Cause at the time I was just worried. Will I play? My mind frame was books, basketball, being happy. The books was coming all right. It was the basketball. My jump shot was off. I didn't have the confidence I have now. Beginning of the school year, I would just come in and shoot. Shoot. Just shoot. It's the way I get if I'm worried about something, stressed out about something, that's what I do, get a basketball, dribble my frustrations out."

His worries vanished like vapor, but not until his first game for North Central, when he hit his first three-pointer in the victory over Anderson. Then he felt right. He was Huggy again on the court.

He was being talked about in Indianapolis as he helped get North Central off on a long winning streak. Penny Dye politely accepted thanks from parents of other North Central players for bringing them Huggy. He'd gotten more press back in Danville. Among the latest articles he'd taped to his bedroom wall was one headlined: "Huggy Dye Living High in Indianapolis."

He was getting the ball enough to suit him, and that's what he loved most, having the ball: "I get the ball, I can do whatever I want. Ain't no stoppin' me. I just get the ball, it's like medicine. I done worked so hard on defense and I've come back down the court and I got the ball in my hands and now I'm going to spend my money."

Huggy attributed his early-season productivity to having practiced in the early hours, when even in Indiana not many kids would be shooting baskets. But he would be there, in the North Central gym. He would be alone with his thoughts, worried, angry, Ben Davis still stuck in his mind, and he was determined to alter civilization as it was known in Indiana high school basketball, imagining going coast-to-coast through a slew of Ben Davis Giants, waiting impatiently for the season and the real Giants, thinking: "I want to show them there's somebody out there always when they're sleeping, somebody out there on the basketball court running suicides, shooting extra free throws, dribbling the ball left-handed up and down the floor, by himself. Night, too. When the lights go off, still out there shootin' for another half an hour. And Mom has to come and pick me up from the floor."

11

A Plea

JANUARY winter hit Indiana with a bitterness that did not relent for days. Snow fell on every inch of the state, thick ice made roads impassable, the temperature plunged to thirteen below. Semi-trailer trucks jackknifed off interstates, country roads vanished under drifts, winds penetrated layers of clothing and flattened road signs. High school basketball games had to be rescheduled because of treacherously slick roads. At the same time arguments to save the single-class high school basketball tournament grew fevered.

Legislators, weather-bound close to the statehouse in Indianapolis, made it to work to take up Indiana's biennial budget and other matters — including basketball, which four lawmakers deemed close to the hearts of their constituents. They filed a bill that would delay the death of the single tournament, maybe even save it, pending a statewide referendum. The Bobby Plump–led group "Friends of Hoosier Hysteria" persuaded the legislators to take the shot against a four-tiered tournament based on school size.

The *Indianapolis Star* urged the bill's passage. In an editorial the newspaper declared that "this battle is not just about basketball, it's about tradition, history and Hoosier values. And it's about respecting the wishes of Indiana citizens, who have loved their high school tournament. . . ."

A few days later Plump and his followers made their way up the steps of the capitol and through its rotunda, where they passed a bust of Lincoln; a sculpture of Wendell Willkie; numerous state-related plaques: "Heroic Hoosier Civil War Citizens," "The Hoosier of the Year" (Gil Hodges, 1955; Kurt Vonnegut, 1974), "The Indiana Mothers Hall of Fame"; and a bronzed poem by William Herschell:

> Ain't God good to Indiana?
> Folks, a feller never knows
> Just how close he is to Eden
> Till, sometimes, he ups and goes
> Seekin' fairer, greener pastures
> Than he has right here at home,
> Where there's sunshine in th' clover
> An' there's honey in th' comb;
> Where th' ripples in th' river
> Kind o' chuckles as they flow —
> Ain't God good to Indiana?
> Ain't He, fellers? Ain't He though?

With an introduction by a lobbyist, Plump arrived at a table of lawmakers who looked harder to read than Muncie Central's defender decades earlier: they were, variously, smiling, poker-faced, slouched. Spectators filled every chair on the sides of the room, others stood. Plump was used to playing to full houses, but in the formal setting of government he squirmed before settling down: "This is the first time I've ever spoken out publicly on an issue. Because there are more people in this room than in my hometown, that makes me nervous."

Marvin Wood, the coach of Milan's 1954 champions, served as top sergeant in Plump's army. If ever somebody fit the image of the best kind of coach, one whose guidance a player craved in the last seconds of a close game, Wood was that person. A man who had twice turned back cancer, he delivered an extemporaneous statement in dulcet tones, measuring each word, that conveyed deep concern that Indiana was about to lose something precious. He'd retired from the game and was living up in Mishawaka, near South Bend. Listening to him, one could imagine the confidence he once communicated to his Milan players.

"I will simply tell you," he said to the legislators, "that I'm from a small town and that I lived for the day when we could compete in our sectional and gain respect. I can tell you that we didn't dream about winning the state championship. We dreamed about competing with our neighbors. I like that idea of the small school competing, giving that small school the chance. I really feel the people make the game what it is. The fans have come to see and support it, and I don't feel they've had a chance to express their opinions yet. The fans have made Indiana basketball what it is.

"I can tell you another thing that disturbs me. It disturbs me when society divides people into classes. I think that's what we're doing. And you know who's making the decision? The higher-ups. The little guy doesn't have a whole lot to say. I'm not a rabble-rouser. I like to be a team player. But I have some pretty strong feelings. And I'm pretty frustrated."

Others used the open forum to echo Wood's sentiments. An executive from the First National Bank of Warsaw, in north-central Indiana, told of his pleasure in beating a larger bank out of a multi-million-dollar contract. John Elliott, senior vice president, likened his bank to the smallest classification in the new Indiana basketball format, 1A, with the beaten bank as a 4A. Compete, don't classify, he said. "Something that has been cherished and honored throughout the years . . . , we are saying, gee, you can't compete. No, we're going to protect you so that you only have to compete against the lower-class level."

Still others pleaded. Then the teams changed sides.

The Indiana High School Athletic Association's executive director, Bob Gardner, testified that the organization had researched the issue thoroughly during the previous two years, and suggested that breaking one class into four would provide "realistic opportunities for young people." School principals and others said it was time for change. "Class sports level the playing field and give more students and their schools a chance to succeed and become state champions," said Bruce Whitehead, athletic director of Crawfordsville High and chairman of the study committee for the IHSAA. Tom Smith, the principal of the Indianapolis school Speedway, portrayed his small school's chance in the annual sectional at Ben Davis with such a hopelessness it would be like a car lined up to start the Indy 500 without an engine.

Three students from Whiting, a small school in the northwestern region, concluded the association's argument against the single tournament with a straightforward message: "We're tired of getting pounded."

The bill's sponsors got the final say. As they were about to wrap up their argument, an older man from Noblesville dressed in work clothes stepped forth. He said he'd been a teacher; he had the delivery of a preacher. His voice filled the chamber in a cry for the preservation of the single tournament. Repeatedly he invoked the names of John Wooden and Jesus. Hoosiers hold both in the highest respect, but this might have been the first cause momentous enough to link both deities in the same breath.

12

Corners of
History

O NE NIGHT early in 1997, players from the 1947 Shelbyville championship team gathered at the school's large domed gym to celebrate their title victory over Terre Haute Garfield, which had been expected to win the championship because it was undefeated and had the huge Clyde Lovellette, a future pro. People in Shelbyville, south of Indianapolis, had invited back their old heroes. Indiana towns never forget their heroes; celebrations take place almost at a whim, but this was a major anniversary — fifty years.

Copies of the *Shelbyville Democrat* of Monday, March 24, 1947, were handed out at the doors. The paper told of "a Saturday night roof-raising which carried into the daylight hours of Sunday morning and left the whole community limp and weary." The paper reported: "A state basketball championship really puts a town on the map! . . . Mayor Jim Pierce received a telephone call early Sunday morning from a *Chicago Tribune* reporter asking for a statement. The mayor told the Windy City newsman: 'I knew we'd win all the time.'"

Fifty years later a full house once more applauded the Golden Bears' glory-days players. Everyone listened to the last minutes of a scratchy radio account of the game. Betty Garrett Inskeep, widow of the team's star Bill Garrett, received a standing ovation and blew a kiss of gratitude from center court. Her husband later had been the first black basketball player in the Big Ten, at Indiana, and then a successful high school coach who took Crispus Attucks of Indianapolis to the 1959 state championship. Bill Garrett Jr., a high school basketball coach in Chicago, wore his father's Shelbyville championship ring, "one of my most cherished possessions." He wondered how his team was doing in its game in Chicago, but there was only one place for him to be that night — in Shelbyville, representing his father.

Everett Burwell, a 1947 player, came in for the reunion from Three Forks, Montana, more than seventeen hundred miles. "If it had been ten thousand miles I'd still have come," he said.

Indianans seem to celebrate high school basketball, one way or another, every week. Another night, in Jasper, a dinner was scheduled for the sole purpose of celebrating the game in general. Coaches and players, the kind who made playing in such small towns seem the biggest thing in the world, assembled at the Knights of Columbus just off the square.

A county seat, Jasper is a gem of a place. The population of about 10,000 doubles daily when people come into work at the factories — which include Kimball, known for pianos but much diversified, and Jasper Engines and Transmissions, a cream-colored building with a mammoth American flag out front. Jasper, virtually spotless, has done away with garbage collection through a municipal program designed to put a garbage grinder in every home.

Bobby Plump was the speaker that night. He warmed up the dinner crowd by recalling the '49 championship game, which foreshadowed his Milan team's upset of '54. Jasper went into the '49 tournament with an 11–9 record. It had a coach called Cabby and a top scorer known as Dimp. Cabby O'Neill and Jerome "Dimp" Stenftenagel. They became part of Indiana lore when they led Jasper to six straight come-from-behind victories en route to the title game against Madison, which they won by a point. "First state tournament I ever remember listening to," said Plump. "We didn't get electricity at my house in Pierceville until 1947. Glenn Butte, who was a sophomore on our team in 1954, and myself were playing in my backyard. One of us was Jasper and one of us was Madison. We had the radio on and the lights going. What excitement. I knew Jasper couldn't win. There wasn't any way, right?" More than 15,000 greeted the winners in the Jasper square.

For the dinner, a display of memorabilia was set up in the back of a large second-floor dining room at the K of C. Visitors paused, told stories in front of the old uniforms and other items: a well-worn Vincennes Lincoln letter jacket, a high school team photograph with Larry Bird in it, yearbooks, the "Little Brown Jug" that for years went to the winner of the annual Jasper-Huntingburg game, a dope bag. A dope bag?

Sinister sounding, it was nothing more than a worn black-leather satchel that a doctor might have toted to a house call. The dope bag used to be a traveling trophy peculiar to southwestern Indiana. The idea was conceived in the 1920s by an Evansville sportswriter. Dope meant information, as in "Who's got the dope on this game?" Schools in eight counties competed for the bag for forty years.

Inside the bag remained a black metal box and within the box two small leather-bound ledger books, their pages yellowed and crumbling, the writing faded. One page listed "six rules for transferring the bag." Jasper set off a weeklong celebration in 1939 when it beat rival Huntingburg, seven miles to the south, in the

117th dope-bag game; Huntingburg had held the bag for a record thirty-five games dating from 1936. Dope-bag games were played from 1929 to 1963, when the bag disappeared. It was discovered ten years later in a filing cabinet and donated to the Indiana Basketball Hall of Fame.

In 1950 Huntingburg achieved a coup at Jasper's expense by completing a 6,214-seat gymnasium even though Huntingburg's population was only 5,376. The structure meant that the town would replace Jasper as host of the tournament sectional. Of the sixty-four sectionals, none was said to be any more anticipated than Huntingburg's. The same was true in 1997. Huntingburg had gained recent notice because of Hollywood films made there. Its bijou baseball park was used as the set for a film about women's baseball, *A League of Their Own*, and in 1996 the town agreed to board up stores on Main Street and have fire hydrants opened to flood a two-block area of downtown for the filming of *Flood*. But Geena Davis and Madonna, ballplayers in *League*, and Randy Quaid, the sheriff in *Flood*, were passing fancies compared with the basketball sectional. A death was the only sure way to free up a ticket.

Denny Lewis, Jasper's athletic director, explained that people would try almost anything to get into a sectional in Huntingburg. A few years ago, for example, he stopped in the men's room before a game and found big bags of ice discarded there. He went to the nearest ticket taker, who told him: "Oh, yeah, three or four guys came through here with ice. Said it was for the sodas."

Imagine the wistfulness in octogenarian Cyril Birge's voice when, contemplating the end of the single tournament, he said: "This season is going to be the last Huntingburg sectional."

Inclined to heritage and nostalgia, Indianans get attached to things. Their still-deep love of autos and auto racing bloomed with the advent of the motorcar in Indiana. Tucked deep in wooded countryside one still came across horse-drawn plows, kerosene lamps, blacksmith shops, homes made of rough planks. One landmark of the heart endured in different form: the gym — a livery stable — that would become home to Wingate High, 1913 and 1914 state champions, still stood. It was now a supply barn for a paper company, its shelves heavy with inventory. A backboard and basket were still in place amid cartons and crates. The Wingate Gymnasium was a monument to the "Gymless Wonders" led by Homer "Stoney" Stonebraker. Stonebraker was six feet four and could throw in shots from great distances; it was part of the game then to shoot from absolutely anywhere on the court. Stonebraker still was considered among the best players by Herb Schwomeyer, whose book *Hoosier Hysteria* is not the only one so titled and whose card described him as "Hoosier Hysteria Historian . . . A Speaker for Any Speaking Situation."

Back in "Stoney's" day, in towns like Wingate and Thorntown, the 1915 champions, teams often practiced outdoors. Most games took place in barns heated by potbellied stoves. Showers — baths, actually — were taken in large galvanized tubs. Crowds for the games made conditions cramped, enthusiasm usually was high, and close contests spawned the term *barn burner*. The state's first eight state champions came from a thirty-mile radius in west-central Indiana. Franklin's "Wonder Five" have been credited with establishing "Hoosier Hysteria" by winning titles in 1920, '21, and '22. The star was "Fuzzy" and the coach "Griz" — Fuzzy Vandivier and Ernest "Griz" Wagner — quintessential Hoosiers.

The first iron hoops in Indiana, forged at a blacksmith's in Crawfordsville, had coffee sacks attached to catch the ball; one of the game's first innovations was to cut the bottoms off the coffee sacks so the ball no longer needed to be pushed out with a pole. The first official game was played in Crawfordsville's YMCA, above a tavern — and a passion for the game ignited there in the midst of Indiana's golden age of literature. Lew Wallace sat out on his front porch in Crawfordsville and wrote parts of *Ben-Hur*. The "Athens of Indiana" was a writers community. James Buchanan Elmore of Crawfordsville was a poet laureate of Indiana. Meredith Nicholson, author of the turn-of-the-century book *The Hoosiers*, wrote: "It pleases me to emphasize Crawfordsville's stimulating atmosphere, the ampler ether and diviner air, which nothing can destroy." A women's literary club, "The Athenian," thrived there. So did a drama club.

"Increasingly in the twentieth century Indianans venerated values and lifestyles they saw as antithetical to urban, industrial America," writes historian James H. Madison in a 1986 book, *The Indiana Way: A State History*. "Their state song ('On the Banks of the Wabash Far Away') and the state poem ('God Crowned Her Hills with Beauty') celebrated wooded hillsides, the smell of new-mown hay, and moonlit rivers." Indiana's high school basketball tournament grew to be such a part of life that a social scientist with no particular interest in sports couldn't help noticing that near the end of winters "through the sycamores the basketballs are flying."

In 1926 Robert and Helen Lynd began work on *Middletown*, a sociological study of a small American city — Muncie, on the flat land between Anderson and Fort Wayne. Muncie High — the Bearcats, later Muncie Central — had not yet won the first of its eight state titles. The first would come in 1928 with a 13–12 victory over defending champion Martinsville, led by John Wooden, then a senior and Purdue-bound. But the Lynds easily discerned basketball's grip on Muncie and beyond. "During the height of the basketball season when all the cities and towns of the state are fighting for the state championship amidst the delirious backing of the rival citizens, the dominance of this sport is as all-pervasive as football in a college like Dartmouth or Princeton the week of the 'big game.' . . . It is the 'Bearcats,' particularly the basketball team, that dominate the life of the school. Friday nights throughout the season are preempted for games."

In their 1937 *Middletown in Transition*, the Lynds observed that the people of Muncie gave gold watches to the basketball team when it won the state championship — in spite of the lingering effects of the Depression. In 1954 Muncie Central was going for a fifth state championship when its title-game opponent turned out to be Milan, a place with just as keen an interest in the game as Muncie.

The week before Milan won its championship an *Indianapolis Times* man reported from downstate: "A critical water shortage perils this Ripley County town of 1,150, but it couldn't care less. It is more concerned about its team in the state basketball finals."

After Plump's last shot Jimmie Angelopolous wrote in the *Indianapolis Times* of the Milan team's triumphant return home: "In Shelbyville, two little boys, one holding a basketball, waved at the champs. Another kid shooting baskets with a little girl outdoors in Greensburg paused to salute the team. A fire truck and police escort screamed sirens at Greensburg. Another fire truck waited at 1 P.M. at Batesville. The procession of cars snowballed by the hundreds entering Ripley County. Traffic slowed behind police and fire truck escort. Hundreds of cars lined the road at Penntown, thirteen miles north of Milan. It took thirty-five minutes to creep eight miles from Batesville to Sunman. Traditional rival Sunman, enrollment 100-plus, was just as proud of its neighbor. It greeted the team with a band reception. Flags lined the street."

To which Plump said in 1997: "We were lucky that Oscar was a sophomore."

In 1954 Milan beat Oscar Robertson's Crispus Attucks in a final-eight game as Plump scored 28 and Robertson 22.

Plump went on to play at Butler University and eventually became an insurance man. Robertson became one of the greatest college and professional players, making most of his fame in Cincinnati, now his home. But first he solidified his reputation as perhaps the best all-round player in Indiana history by leading Crispus Attucks to its state championships of 1955 and '56. For the first time an all-black school dominated the state. America was changing.

Robertson wished the change had been faster. "As I've grown older and have been able to look back at those times, I can't believe the way we were treated," Robertson was quoted by Kerry Marshall in a biography of Attucks coach Ray Crowe, *A Legend in High School Basketball.* "I find myself asking: What right did those white people have to treat us so poorly? To be honest, there are things about Indianapolis that I remember that no one should have in his memory. The bigotry and racism I saw was not always done in ignorance. Some of it was intentional. Those experiences have tarnished what should have been some of the better days of my life."

Crowe, eighty-one, lives in an apartment in northwest Indianapolis with a den full of photographs of his Crispus Attucks teams and a large photo of a statue of Robertson that was unveiled in 1994 at his alma mater, the University of Cincinnati. "Oscar's bitter about some of the things that happened during that time," said Crowe, a state representative and Indianapolis city councilman after his coaching days. One thing that angered Robertson was the location of Attucks's championship celebrations — Indianapolis city officials arranged for them to be held in a park in a black section of the city rather than where blacks and whites might celebrate together. Crowe didn't concur on that but agreed wholeheartedly on this: "Most of the referees were white referees and we got a lot of bad calls. There was a lot of bigotry and racism shown right out there on the floor. We could see it. I could tell it. Oscar could tell. But I tried to get him to overcome that and build up the lead so the referees couldn't make the difference."

Rick "The Rocket" Mount was Indiana's hotshot of the sixties at both Lebanon and Purdue, but his pro career in the American Basketball Association was a cooler time. He retired early. "I still loved the game of basketball," he told Bob Williams in his book called *Hoosier Hysteria!,* "but I didn't enjoy all of the other things about the pro scene. Pro ball is nothing like high school and college — it's a job and too much of a cutthroat proposition. Coach [Jim] Rosenstihl recognized my talents and let me do what I could do best — shoot the ball. They tried to make a ballhandling guard out of me when I went to the pros."

Mount's professional days seemed an interruption to practicing his life's art, the jump shot. Now, a quarter century after his prime, Mount still is in Lebanon, still shooting jump shots, the concert pianist playing at home for his own satisfaction.

But life in Indiana was hardly as bucolic as depicted in Mount's heyday. An auto plant in South Bend had shut down. On a gray December day in 1963 the Studebaker Corporation announced it was ending auto production there after sixty-one years. So much for an Indiana landmark and "Craftsmanship with a flair," a Studebaker motto. According to *Time:* "Workers poured from the plant in shock and anger." Northern Indianans, engaged in heavy industry, lost jobs for more than a decade. Gary's steel mills laid off one-third of their workers — some 22,000 — in a single month in 1971.

That year, 1971, was the last time the state's high school basketball tournament was played in the grand field house at Butler. George McGinnis was happy to have had his "dream come true," playing there and winning the title, in 1969, just in time. He and Steve Downing led Indianapolis Washington to an undefeated season. "Indiana high school basketball meant everything to me," said McGinnis. "Looking back, there was never any feeling I ever had like winning the high school tournament. I played on an ABA championship team, was the most valuable player in a basketball league. I was the first sophomore to lead the Big Ten in rebounding and scoring. But never have I been able to recapture that feeling of winning the state tournament."

From 1928 through 1971, with the exception of three years during World War II, the finals took place in the Butler arena now named for Tony Hinkle. Hinkle is one of the immortals of college coaching, and Butler was the place where teams from the west got off trains to play on their way to New York's Madison Square Garden. Hinkle built Butler's basketball reputation, but his first love was Indiana high school basketball. It was the source of much of his talent. "When we were kids," McGinnis said, "a friend of mine was just old enough to get a car, so we could get around.

We drove to Butler and sat in the car and did a mock radio play-by-play of the championship game with us in it."

Hinkle Fieldhouse is a massive brick building with a curved roof on the edge of the Butler campus in Indianapolis's comfortable northern section. Walk in and there's a smell of age and must. Pull back a blue curtain and one is standing at a corner of the court. Boys are shooting baskets.

"It's the greatest floor in the world to play on, yet today," said Marvin Cave, former player and coach and currently president of the Indiana Basketball Hall of Fame. "You get on it and it's got a soft bounce and so — whether you can dunk or not, and in the old days not too many could — it feels like you can just go up h-i-i-gher than you really can. That floor is so great, always has been."

Hollywood didn't have to change a thing for *Hoosiers*. All the steel and iron give Hinkle the look of a sports museum, a treasure. Now the seats closest to the court are chairs made of aluminum, but the rows in back are still wood benches. They're worn, dented. They wrap behind both baskets and sweep far up on a gentle slope toward large windows near the roof. Fans turn in the ceiling.

When the place was quiet, one could sit there on an afternoon and easily imagine the black-and-white film, sometimes jerky, sometimes blurry, of Plump dribbling away the last seconds in 1954 and the play-by-play voice screaming above the roaring crowd, "Can you hear me out there? Can you hear me out there?"

Batesville's Michael Menser holds a piece of the net from the 1997 Ripley County tourney.

Mike Fender, *Indianapolis Star*

Menser on the move against New Castle in a 1997 regional tournament game.

Bryan Helvie, *Batesville Herald-Tribune*

Batesville students love their Bulldogs.

Mike Fender, *Indianapolis Star*

Coaches at work. Merrillville's Jim East, Ben Davis's Steve Witty (with James Patterson in the 1995 title game), and Batesville's Melvin Siefert.

East and Witty by Mark Wick, courtesy of the Indiana High School Athletic Association. Siefert by Randy Amick.

Anderson's Ron Hecklinski leads his team in prayer before a game at Noblesville.

Perry Reichanadter, *Anderson Herald Bulletin*

The family. Ron answers a reporter's question as his wife, Pam, and daughter, Stephanie, wait.

Perry Reichanadter, *Anderson Herald Bulletin*

Hecklinski queries an official during Anderson's season-ending loss to Delta in the tournament regional.

Perry Reichanadter, *Anderson Herald Bulletin*

An inconsolable Eric Bush anguishes at midcourt in the Wigwam as Delta celebrates its upset victory over Anderson's fifth-ranked Indians.

Perry Reichanadter,
Anderson Herald Bulletin

A pair of aces. DeKalb's Recker and Batesville's Menser played for the Indiana all-stars in their two postseason games with the Kentucky all-stars. Recker wore the coveted number 1 as Indiana's "Mr. Basketball."

Bryan Helvie, *Batesville Herald-Tribune*

Mike Fender, *Indianapolis Star*

13

Games

J ANUARY 4. Batesville was 9–0 and climbing steadily in the
polls. On this Saturday night the team played in Kokomo.
Superior Street, which runs along one wall of Kokomo's
Memorial Gymnasium, was hardly wider than the big white-
and-blue bus that inched its way to the curb. The bus door
swung open and Batesville's players filed off. Two strides
across the sidewalk and they were in the side door and almost on
the court, already looking around, looking up at the maze of
girders and light bulbs in the ceiling. "State of the art, 1947,"
said Jim Callane, Kokomo's athletic director, by way of welcome
to what was clearly an admirable building.

Rows of seats stretched high into ever dimmer light. Four steel
posts, set back from the court's four corners, helped support the
roof but blocked the view of anyone sitting behind them. In the
fifties and sixties Memorial Gym was filled every game, which

meant a raucous crowd of almost 7,000. Kokomo won the state title in 1961. "In the sixties you got a season ticket to half the games," said Callane. "You couldn't get a ticket to the whole season unless you were politically connected."

Callane turned to Batesville coach Melvin Siefert.

"Our attendance has fallen off," he said.

"Our last game we were full," said Siefert, hastening to suggest that Batesville might lack the array of activities available in Kokomo. "There are so many distractions here," he said. "What else do you do in Batesville?"

Near the gymnasium's front door was an elegant room, atypical of gyms. Wood paneled, with leather sofas and chairs, it served as a memorial to an army officer, John E. Turner, and others killed in World War II. Three stained-glass windows honored the U.S. Army, Navy, and Marines, and gave the room the feel of a chapel.

Fans passing through the room on the way to their seats could read a plaque: "This memorial conceived in loving memory and enduring gratitude is dedicated to those promising sons who grew to young manhood in our homes and schools of Howard County and who, mindful only of duty to their country and loved ones, offered their lives and all else they possessed that liberty, justice and individual freedom might be enjoyed by future generations. . . ."

The room also contained, in a departure from the rest of the decor, a plastic case with a stuffed wildcat. The Kokomo team is known as the Wildkats, with a k. On game nights cheerleaders take the wildcat in the case and place it at midcourt while the two teams warm up, then return it to its hallowed space.

In a matter of moments Michael Menser was dressed in his warm-ups and out on the court shooting around, to be joined one by one by his Batesville teammates. Menser was there to play, not to inhale the setting, and his first business was testing the rims.

Siefert had scheduled this game as a test for his team. By chance he and Basil Mawbey, Kokomo's coach, had been playing golf together six months before and Mawbey, who had an open date, invited Siefert to bring his team to Kokomo. Batesville almost never traveled out of southern Indiana, but Siefert canceled an easy game and accepted because he wanted to see how his team would react "in front of a hostile crowd."

In addition, Kokomo had a notorious reputation throughout the state as a place where officiating for some reason seemed to favor the home team more than in most places. Anderson's Johnny Wilson said: "They ought to spot you fifteen points when you play in Kokomo."

This night, the crowd was swelled by more than a thousand Batesville fans who had found their way to the "City of Firsts." Kokomo boasted an array of "firsts," from bomb shells used in World War I to the mechanical corn picker to canned tomato juice. A car made by Elwood Haynes made the first successful automobile run in the United States on Pumpkinville Pike in 1894. It chugged along at six miles per hour.

Kokomo, named for a Miami Indian chief, greets visitors with a string of stoplights on U.S. 31 and a natural gas tower dominating the skyline. Memorial Gym is located a block north of Wildcat Creek, on which the city was built despite one early cynic's forecast that because of flooding and dense underbrush "a more unpromising place to build a town cannot well be imagined." Mawbey, who coached Connersville to the state title in 1983, put new life into Kokomo in 1989 when he coached the Kats to state runner-up, losing the title game to Indianapolis's Lawrence North, led by Eric Montross. Three years later Mawbey needed triple bypass heart surgery, but he returned to the bench within a few months and had continued to frustrate opponents with "Basil Ball."

Mawbey taught a methodical offense — many passes each possession — and a zone defense that sometimes looked as if it wasn't going to work but usually did. Sometimes, having lulled the opposition, he would reverse tactics late in a game — push the ball up the court quickly and play man-to-man defense. And win. The irony in Batesville's playing Kokomo was that the bigger team from the city wanted to slow the game against the little school from the country.

Batesville dressed for the occasion in its new road blue uniforms, which gave it the look of Duke. Menser in particular looked as if he'd been born to play for Duke, with its history of diminutive but tenacious perimeter shooters. Jenny Menser sat halfway up in the stands; Jim Menser sat near the top. Unlike his wife, Jim Menser was spare with words in the course of a game. He was one of those people with whom it almost isn't necessary to speak during a play — an exchanged glance, a shrug or gesture said enough.

He pointed out two of the state's top players sitting in the stands, friends of Michael who'd come from nearby to see him play, Nick Wise of Plymouth — the Pilgrims — and Caleb Springer of Logansport — the Berries. Like Menser, they looked like cherubs. But they all were toughened as much as anything by basketball competition and by structured home life. Springer was born at home, as were his siblings, because his mother didn't want to bother with hospitals; two hours after delivering Caleb she was in the kitchen cooking breakfast.

Mike Menser was not awed to be in Kokomo. He'd played Las Vegas. The previous summer he was there as a member of the Bloomington Red AAU team. In the Nike/Las Vegas Invitational tournament's title game, Bloomington Red routed Team Brooklyn, 97–67. Luke Recker scored 20; Menser had 12 with eight assists. What Hoosier fan wouldn't delight to a backcourt with Menser at the point and Recker at shooting guard? "Mike Menser, he's a great player," said Recker. "People look at him and say, 'What is he, five seven? He's not a player.' I would love playing with Michael all the time. He's so tough. He's going to be so tough for Indiana State."

Against Kokomo, Menser scored the game's first points with a quick-hands play. A Kat grabbed a rebound, but Menser swiped the ball and threw in a jump shot from the baseline almost before anyone else had moved. Batesville found Kokomo's pace tedious but adjusted enough to take a 25–13 lead. Batesville's rooters loved it; the home crowd was quiet. A few minutes into the third quarter Kokomo switched to a pressing man-to-man defense and began to rally. Jim Menser, unlike most parents watching their children play in a game, maintained a rare calm even as the lead began to slip. Matter-of-factly he observed: "Batesville is playing like Kokomo is still in a zone, instead of going to the basket."

With two and a half minutes to play Menser the younger was trying to run out the clock when surrounded by three frantic Kats. The whistle sounded. Foul on the play. It was called against . . . Menser! It was an official's call that conjured thoughts of the late Johnny Most, whose raspy voice brought the Boston Celtics' play-by-play: "They've got Sharman surrounded. They're pounding on Sharman. They're beating him to death. There's the whistle. What? I don't believe it! The foul's on Sharman!"

Batesville led the entire game — except for the last two seconds. The Kats took a 42–41 lead by converting the second of two offensive rebounds. Batesville called time. Menser would take the inbounds pass and fling a shot from three-quarter court. The outcome was all but sealed, but because Menser was playing, not quite. Memorial Gymnasium fell hushed, everyone stood. Time was in. Menser squirted free — a feat because he was surrounded again — and got the ball. Immediately he let it fly. The horn sounded but the ball stayed aloft and continued soaring past the girders in a trajectory that looked dreamily true. Everyone stood watching. The scene looked like a painting or photograph.

The ball hit the back of the rim — so close — and fell softly away.

A roar went up and Kokomo students swarmed the court.

Jim Menser shrugged and smiled.

Little Batesville was moving up in status in Indiana basketball. Its defeat was cause for an opponent's celebration.

Later, Michael Menser sat alone in the stands. Almost everyone had left. He stared at the court, contemplating the defeat, his face solemn and pale beneath a blue cap. He'd scored 16, even had four rebounds. But he looked sad, the way Eric Bush had after Batesville upset Anderson at the Hall of Fame Classic. Later Menser said: "I felt terrible, like the world dropping out from under me."

Just because of a loss?

"We were up by six with two and a half minutes to go. We turned it over. We missed shots. We played well enough to win. We didn't execute down the stretch the way we have in the past. We blew it."

He still was staring when Kokomo's Jim Callane climbed up to him, put a hand on his shoulder, and guided him to a room where pizza was served.

After that, the Batesville players walked out to their bus. They were silent, their heads bent. It was raining. They had come thinking they would win and, until the last two seconds of the game, kept that thought. They would think about how they'd lost for the rest of this Saturday night as they headed south toward home.

January 11. Anderson was 8–2 and ranked eighth in the state media poll and eleventh in the coaches' poll. The Indians met Bloomington North, number five in both polls, at the Wigwam.

Hecklinski had been totally exhausted when Pam drove him back to Anderson after the loss to Batesville in the Hall of Fame Classic. It had been a difficult day for him, too long a day with the doubleheader. That night, after the loss and his locker-room tirade, the circles under his eyes were deep, his voice more hoarse than usual. Fortunately, he now had a break in the schedule, which would give him virtually two weeks of rest. His physical condition clearly had limited him. Some days he felt better, and could coach better, than others. He knew the players sensed it.

"He's so distant now," said Eric Bush, sitting disconsolately on a bench in the locker room after practice one day. "He used to play with us and practice with us. He's not that vocal anymore. He seems to let a lot of stuff get by him."

Before his surgery, Hecklinski had been like a performer who turns on when the lights go up. At practices he not only would shout instructions but underscore them with his whole being — a couple of long, quick steps would shoot him right up to a player's face to make sure he got that player's attention. During games his inner fires would ignite, and he would lift off the bench and land almost in the game; while his feet would be planted at the court's edge, the upper half of his long body leaned forward over the court. He'd be after somebody — a player, a ref. He was an all-systems-go overseer.

Bush had never seen Hecklinski in reflective poses, seated at practice. No one pictured Heck as "The Thinker."

Now the break without games helped him. He began to feel stronger. He'd been "pissed" by the loss to Batesville and got rid of his chair at practice. He got back out on the court and his voice resounded again in the empty Wigwam. He managed this by limiting most of his daily activity to the practices. He was gaining confidence that he would survive a year, then the five years that Van Thiel had said would put him "probably on a normal survival course."

"I feel real good about my coaching," he said in January. "It's the first time all season I've felt good about my coaching."

He looked better — his eyes were bright, his face had more color — when he walked into his office before a Saturday night game against Bloomington North. This was going to be as difficult as the Hall of Fame games because Bloomington North was a rising power that had won 21 straight regular-season games. The school had an array of foreign students and several on the basketball team. Most of their parents lived in Bloomington because they were affiliated with Indiana U. in some way; many were pursuing advanced degrees. Bloomington North's best player was six-foot-five

Kueth Duany from the Sudan, whose older brother Duany Duany played for Wisconsin. Djibril Kante, six six, came from Mali. Other players were from Indonesia and the Philippines. All were combining to give the city of Bloomington a cachet in high school basketball as well as in college ball.

Conversations about Bloomington usually included some mention of Bob Knight. "He called me about three weeks before I had the surgery," said Hecklinski. "He assumed that I was going to have this done at the I.U. Medical Center and I had to tell him on the phone, 'Well, no, Coach, I'm having it done at your favorite place, the University of Kentucky.' And after a few expletives he said, 'You gotta be kidding me.'

"Then he sent me two really nice letters at Lexington, which I hung up on the wall, so that the Kentucky nurses and doctors could get a kick out of that. After I was home for a week or so a friend drove me to Bloomington to go to an I.U. practice. First thing, [Knight] calls me 'Eddie Sutton,'" a reference to the former Kentucky coach. "'What the hell's Eddie Sutton doing here?'

"We had a nice conversation. I personally think it would be good for Eric to be there with a guy who would be hard on him but who would care about him. That's the thing about Coach Knight — he's so caring. But he cares about you in such a way that you might not think he cares about you. But if you ever need anything, he's right there for you. Who am I to him, really, and here he is right on the phone saying, 'What can I do for you?'"

Johnny Wilson called Hecklinski "the Bobby Knight of high school coaches," not because he was as explosive as Knight but because Wilson admired Knight's coaching and agreed with most of what Knight had to say. But Hecklinski could lose it periodically. The Hecklinski incident that brought to mind the episode when Knight threw a chair in a game happened during the 1984–85 season when Hecklinski coached at Jasper. During a practice he got so angry he threw a game clock to the floor and smashed it. For that he was called into the principal's office.

"I've grown up since then," he said. Pause. "If I threw a clock now, I'd be sure to catch it."

He was feeling feisty again, telling stories as he skimmed through an article on himself in Bloomington's *Herald-Times* leading up to the Bloomington North game. "Yep, yep, that's right, they got it right. That's good, good article. . . . Now I gotta get to work."

Once the Bloomington North game began he was up off the bench, lunging toward the edge of the court, shouting to Bush: "You better tell these guys to guard somebody because they've had twelve possessions and scored on nine of 'em." Bush's face brightened. He'd been anxious to hear some stern directive. He wheeled toward his teammates, yelling, "Hey, you guys, pick up the defense. Let's go. . . ."

Again Hecklinski used his liver condition in working an official: "Hey, I've just had a transplant. Could we get a call here?" The official ignored him.

It was a tense game, one of Anderson's best of the season. Bush failed to score in the first half but got 23 after that — including overtime. Senior Aaron Boyd added 18 and Anderson won, 81–76. For Bush, the best thing was that Hecklinski seemed to be himself. "He's finally back out there coaching," Bush said. "He's being aggressive with us and everything. We want that. We know it's got to be business. We want to do better than last year. We want to win it all."

January 16. Surprising North Central was 11–0 and ranked number one in the state. This cold Thursday night brought two-time defending champion Ben Davis, ranked second with a 9–1 record, to North Central's Eighty-sixth Street gym in Indianapolis for a Marion County tournament game. Only four times in the 1990s had Indiana's two top-ranked teams played; the last time was the 1995 state title game, when Ben Davis beat Merrillville.

Ten days later North Central and Ben Davis would meet again on the same court for a regular-season game.

North Central's building was so sprawling it comfortably held its 3,070 students. "We're reflecting the kind of athletic prowess we should have," said Chuck Jones, the athletic director. He was just inside the door of a new gym that seated about 3,000. The old one had been destroyed in a December 1994 fire. These were happier times; he showed off the new arena from a mid-level aisle as people crowded in early for a game that had been the talk of Indianapolis for days. Jones spoke assuredly of North Central's chances — for that night and the rest of the season. Did he believe North Central could win the state championship? Quick smile, quick reply: "Oh, yeah."

Shortly, his confidence was illustrated. North Central's players came out in black warm-ups with a swagger-trot. First, they ran around the perimeter of the court. Then, in step, they assumed a formation and warmed up with a passing drill, whipping the ball back and forth across the width of the floor. Shooting around, they rarely missed. Their coach, Doug Mitchell, a former assistant at Butler, later summarized his game philosophy: "We want to make it as crazy as possible without throwing the ball out the door."

The craziness wasn't just on the court. At North Central human voices and electronic pulsations melded into the thunder roar of rocketry. It was the noisiest gym in all of Indiana.

The place had a sound system that blasted "techno" club music in combination with assorted pandemonium-inducing detonations: the recorded Panther growl (the school's nickname is the Panthers, and the sound of a roaring lion had been borrowed from Penn State); the inescapable Michael Buffer recording, with his "Let's get ready to rumble . . ."; a fifty-piece pep band, including one member, indistinguishable by sex, wearing a pot on his or her head and striking it with a metal object; cheerleaders, whose synchronized freneticism rated seventh in the country during a recent competition in Dallas; the "Hecklers," at least forty male students, most with painted bare chests, two painted like a roaring fire; the Pantherettes, a halftime dance group; a hyperactive fellow dressed as a Panther.

It looked like an MTV music video in the making.

Then there were Jack and Dave.

That would be Jack Gangstad, the public address announcer, and Dave Mock, who operated the sound system. Both were assistant football coaches.

"We want that home-court advantage," said Jack.

"You gotta be able to put some amps out," said Dave.

Dave could. He worked from a room, just off the court, that looked like mission control. He had the music tapes in there, and used a heavy hand on the volume when playing whatever fit the moment, or whatever didn't: "The Final Countdown," "Get Ready 4 This," "Pump Up the Volume," "Atomic Dog," "Y.M.C.A.," "Rock 'n' Roll All Nite," "Rock 'n' Roll, Parts 1 and 2" — the "Hey" song — "Respect," "Twist and Shout," "Mony Mony," "What I Like about You," and, as part of the finale, "Celebration."

Dave, the Leonard Bernstein of north Indianapolis teen life, could look out his door and coordinate with the band and the cheerleaders. He directed a symphony in which no sour note could be detected. In fact, if everyone came in together — Dave on the sound system, the band, the cheerleaders — so much the better. As it was, Dave had no control over the "Hecklers," the leaping Panther, and numerous sign wielders, one of whom waved his message in the face of a Ben Davis player standing at the end of a warm-up line: "Welcome to the jungle."

In its previous game, North Central took a 41–7 halftime lead over Indianapolis Lutheran, and cleared the bench. "We always like to get everyone into the game," said Huggy Dye, whom people were wondering about more and more as big numbers continued to appear alongside his name in the box scores. Who was this Huggy?

Jason Gardner, a sophomore guard, and Dye were North Central's principal forces. Mitchell already was touting Gardner for "Mr. Basketball," 1999. Bob Knight would attend a Marion County tournament game between North Central and Lawrence North, presumably because Tom "Big County" Geyer of Lawrence North was headed to I.U. But Geyer was on the bench injured. Knight, it could be assumed, had eyes for Jason Gardner.

Gardner and Dye both had shaved heads, and both could fire three-pointers with artful touches. But they had different games.

Huggy, it was quickly obvious as the Ben Davis game began, had flair, even brazenness. Talent, too. "Huggy believes he can beat Michael Jordan — that's Huggy," said his mother, Penny Dye.

But for all of Huggy's show, this was Gardner's team even though he was only a sophomore. He was five feet eleven, 175 pounds, and he could easily be envisioned among the premier high school guards in the nation in two years — if not already. He could shoot, drive to the basket, play defense. He was sturdy, faster even than Dye. It would be hard to name a player at any level of the game with a faster first step than Jason Gardner.

North Central sprinted to a 51–42 lead with 5:29 left, playing as crazily fast as Mitchell had said they would. But North Central let Ben Davis back into the game by missing nine free throws in the fourth period. With 26 seconds left, Ben Davis had to foul one time too many. Even before a teammate finally made a free throw to clinch the game, Dye, sensing victory, laughed heartily. A long three-pointer by Ben Davis made the 63–62 final score closer than the game had been. Gardner scored 22, Dye 14. Batesville's Melvin Siefert was in the crowd because if Batesville made it to the Indianapolis semistate in the tournament it likely would play North Central or Ben Davis. Could his team beat North Central? Siefert exhaled. "Not if they play that way," he said. He would have to get the pace slowed, Kokomo-like.

Defeated Ben Davis coach Steve Witty sat on a bench in the locker room. He was perspiring. He'd been prowling in front of his bench all night, commanding, entreating; he'd been down on one knee using every second of his time-outs to impart strategy. To no avail. But his competitive juices prompted him to point out that Ben Davis had been beaten in the county tournament the previous year, then prevailed against the same team in the only tournament that counted, the state tournament.

Ten days later, North Central and Ben Davis resumed battle. Ben Davis, having been knocked out of the county tournament, had been practicing. North Central had improved its record to 14–0 after taking the county tournament by winning two more games. The two games had to be played in one day because of a weather postponement. With ice on the roads, it practically took a luge to get around. When everyone finally made it to Southport Field-house in Indianapolis, Dye was all sizzle in the double victory. He scored 28 points in the first game, 27 at night. In those two games combined he hit 22 of 27 field goal attempts — 82 percent!

Moments before the second North Central–Ben Davis game, North Central's public address announcer pleaded to the crowd: "Squeeze in as close as you can so everybody can see the great game tonight."

What followed was everything anyone would want in a game. The drama and tension grew until the score was tied at 57 with three and a half minutes to play. It was up-and-down-the-floor desperation on both sides — until Dye broke the tie for good. He did this with a three-pointer, holding his pose for effect after the shot. Then he hit another three and North Central was off on a 14–0 run. When he scored on a breakaway layup to make it 65–59 the public address announcer cried: "Huggy Dye, Huggy Dye, Huggy Dye."

The final was 74–62. If the teams were to meet a third time it would be at Hinkle Fieldhouse in the state tournament's Indianapolis regional. In the limp-bodied aftermath of the just-ended encounter, it was reasonable to say that no two teams could have expended greater effort to win a game.

The next night they both lost.

14

End of an Era

THE LAST days of single-class basketball cast a gloom on Indiana to match the cold rain. One morning at Gary Roosevelt, a tall man made his way swiftly along a crowded corridor as classes were beginning. He looked full of energy as he exchanged cheery hellos with students. It wasn't until he'd reached his office, closed the door, and sat down that Ron Heflin suddenly looked tired. He had been coaching for thirty-seven years, twenty-two as Roosevelt's head coach. But he felt worn out. These would be his final days as a coach.

"I was going to retire anyway, but with class basketball coming on, it pushed me more on the side of retiring," he said. "I don't like it. I'm a traditionalist. I thought it made Indiana unique. But we live in a democracy and this is what the majority wants, the majority that makes the rules. So I'll live with it."

A black coach in an all-black school, Heflin was further dismayed. "This was an opportunity, as long as they were changing things, to diversify. But they chose not to. My biggest complaint is the way they realigned for the sectional. The minorities of Gary, Hammond, and East Chicago will be in one sectional. It's going to be a big sectional, a meat grinder out of which only one predominantly black school can emerge.

"You've heard of the Golden Rule? I say you've got to have the gold to make the rules. They've got the gold, they made the rules."

It was pouring rain, the kind of winter day when even the most enduring Hoosiers can feel nerves fraying from the weeks of cold and dismal weather. At this time of year Indianans like to drive to places like Florida and the Gulf Coast of Alabama. Heflin had never taken a winter vacation in the South because he was always coaching. His team usually was in a tournament at Christmastime. But already he was planning a holiday for the next winter. "I'm in dire need," he said.

Because he was only fifty-eight, Heflin said he might return to coaching sometime, but he doubted it — Indiana coaches are all teachers, so their workdays can reach extraordinary lengths. "I teach night classes, as well," he said, "so I don't get home for dinner until almost 11 o'clock. There's not much time before you start all over again." Basketball, the aspect of his life that he would remember most, was only part of his daily routine.

He'd never had a losing season, averaged almost twenty victories, made three final-four coaching appearances, and coached the 1991 title winners with star player Glenn Robinson. Robinson grew up across the street from Roosevelt, and Heflin developed Robinson's game. "When young he didn't play basketball that much. Consequently when I got him I didn't have to break any bad habits. We taught him the right way, not flashy, but fundamentally sound. And then he plays so darn hard; he always had that burning desire and I saw that at an early age — he wanted to accomplish and he did."

Heflin knew Jamaal Davis well. "Jamaal has great potential. The biggest thing Jamaal has to do is improve his work habits. He has the tools, no doubt about that. But now, is he willing to run through a brick wall to refine what God gave him naturally? Right now that separates him from Glenn at the same age. He's got to work a lot harder. I tell Jamaal that myself."

Jamaal, he said, was that rare youngster whose basketball talent could take him to the pros — if he worked and if he were lucky. In Gary, Heflin said, it was becoming less likely for kids to find a future of some kind in basketball — interest in the sport was down, he said, primarily because of a lack of funds for coaches in the middle schools and grade schools. Fewer coaches, he said, meant fewer opportunities for kids to connect with an adult who might inspire them in basketball or some other way.

"We teach life here," Heflin said. "The thing is, of all the great ballplayers I've had, and I've had some real good ballplayers, only two played basketball for a living, Winston Garland, who played eight years in the NBA, and Glenn. So what are the other ninety-nine percent going to do? They've got to go to some community, earn a living, and be productive citizens. Kids have to understand that. My thing has been to develop these kids, get them to conform more to life."

Some still wanted to play basketball at Roosevelt, and some of those dreamed of being a champion like Robinson, the best in Indiana, and those desires and dreams had given Heflin the chance to capitalize and to teach. "That's all I ever wanted," he said, "to teach."

Plymouth, a quiet place, is halfway across the northern part of the state from Gary, but linked by more than U.S. 30. Plymouth and Roosevelt were bound in Indiana basketball history by the 1982 championship game. Scott Skiles scored 39 points for Plymouth in its 75–74 double-overtime victory; his biggest shot was a 22-

footer as time expired to send the game into its first overtime. That victory made Plymouth the only state champion since Milan with fewer than a thousand students in the school.

Jack Edison, a slender, baldish man, was Plymouth's coach then and now. The end of single class saddened him because it had been so much a part of his life growing up near South Bend. Even in middle age he kept to the ideal that "anything you believe, you can achieve — I'm just a believer in this. I don't like to put limits on kids."

He remembered being nine years old when Plump made his shot, twelve when he rooted for South Bend Central to win the state title, which it did. "I put their pictures from the *South Bend Tribune* up at home. I kept things about them in a box for a long time." He played for Greene Township High School, enrollment less than two hundred; when his school was eliminated in the tournaments, he rooted for the sectional winners. "They represented me, that's how I felt," he said. "I don't think I would have traded that dream or hope of winning a sectional game, to pull off a sectional upset against a big team. As a coach, I've always enjoyed the challenge of knocking off the bigger schools. Winning the state championship was quite an experience. As a kid, you win the state championship in your mind. When it happens in reality you realize what a far-off dream it had been."

He sat in a room off to the side of the gym, the site of the Plymouth sectional. He knew that smaller schools Plymouth would face had the same feelings he'd known as a player at a small high school. "You're a target in the sectional," he said. "They all want to beat you. It's where most of the pressure is in the tournament. The biggest problem in dealing with it is that sometimes players and coaches unknowingly change their approach from the season. Lose and you're gone, so you play not to lose. That happens so much at the sectional level."

An old red Plymouth number 22 jersey hung in the trophy case in the lobby — Scott Skiles's jersey. Rick Skiles, Scott's father, standing in the lobby, now was the school's custodian. Scott had moved on to Michigan State and the pros, and was coaching in Greece. Rick had stayed in Plymouth; he was there nightly to slap the hands of the Pilgrims before they took the court. "It's everybody's dream in Indiana to win a state championship," he said. "Scott had that dream even when he was very small. I hope the four class winners could have a playoff. That's what I hope it comes to. That way the small school can still get there."

The full-size figure in the glass case of the school's hallway was difficult to identify, but at least it was labeled: John Wooden. If that was Wooden, this had to be Martinsville, home of the Artesians. Wooden played on three straight title-game teams for the south-central Indiana school from 1926 through '28, including the championship team of '27. He was a three-time All-American at Purdue, then coached at South Bend Central High and Indiana State before moving to UCLA.

One of the games fixed in Wooden's memory was a defeat suffered in the Hammond semistate by his 1941 South Bend Central team. It came on a desperation half-court shot. Wooden thought his team had beaten Gary Froebel High, but that's how it had been so often in the single-class tournament in Indiana: when a team thought it was going to win, it lost. That's what Martinsville's coach, Tim Wolf, and Steve Hardin, a doctor in town who played at Butler for Tony Hinkle, were discussing this day in 1997 in Wolf's office. The school is located in a neighborhood away from Route 37, where many of the businesses are located, including Larry Bird Ford. A sign that students had put up in the hallway read, "THE SECTIONALS ARE OURS." But the two men were saying that no one could be certain, not in the sectionals in Indiana.

"We were number one in the state in 1989–90 and we were upset in the sectional by Bloomington South," said Wolf. "It was absolutely awful. It was devastating. Last year Monrovia won the sectional. It was a given that they didn't have a chance. Enrollment 420. They beat Mooresville. The night before, Mooresville beat us — that was supposed to be the game. Mooresville was expected to beat Monrovia in a cakewalk.''

Hardin added, ''And Monrovia almost upset Terre Haute North the next week in the regional. They were tied with three minutes to go. . . . I think everybody who has grown up in the one-class system would like to see it continue. Every kid in Indiana used to grow up hoping to play in Hinkle Fieldhouse — in the regional, semistate, or state final. But sometimes change comes.''

Wolf, in a more resistant mood, said, ''They call this progress. But Hinkle used to be your goal. Hinkle was the biggest place in the state of Indiana. Hinkle was tradition. It still is. Martinsville played at the Hinkle semistate in 1989 and Hinkle himself'' — then in his nineties — ''spoke to the teams.''

Hardin slipped into rhapsody on Rick Mount. ''I played against him at Butler. He could score anytime he wanted.''

''Best shooter in the history of basketball,'' said Wolf. Then, snapping back to the present, he added, ''This is the last time we'll have a sectional here — the last one. I can't imagine this happening.''

Red-brick Evansville Bosse, in the southwest-corner city, has the look of a school in England's countryside. Its football stadium, posts supporting the roof, resembles a small English soccer stadium. But basketball was Bosse's game — Bosse won state titles in 1944, '45, and '62, and in '82 lost in the final four to Gary Roosevelt, 58–57, on a layup at the buzzer. Bosse usually fielded one of the best teams in Indiana, and it had good prospects for the immediate future. But as matters stood, those prospects would be playing in Class 4A, to no one's pleasure at Bosse.

''As a single human being you don't have the power to change things,'' said Joe Mullan, the former head coach who had been called out of retirement to help as an assistant. He'd played on Evansville North's 1967 championship team.

It was another day of rain. The Ohio River, which snakes past Evansville, was rising, but the city walls were high and solid.

"I don't think winning a championship is going to have the same meaning, the same value as it did," said Mullan. "Growing up, all I ever thought about was playing in the tournament, and when I got to high school my dream was to play in the state finals — and I did, with Dave Schellhase. I consider myself one of the most fortunate people in Indiana to have played in the state finals. I've been able to experience a lot of things. I played Division One basketball and traveled all over the United States. But being Hoosier-bred it comes right back to participating in the state finals. It's the biggest thrill I've ever had as a human being."

Alexandria had only 576 students, but Garth Cone, Alexandria's coach for twenty-one years, was known in Indiana as a master of the upset. Alexandria won the Anderson sectional in 1994 and '95, and the Anderson regional of '95 as well. That day, about 3,000 of the 5,000 people in town went off to Anderson. Someone put up a sign in Alexandria: "Last one out, turn off the lights."

"I think our society is trying to have more winners, and in the attempt to have more winners we're diluting the prize," Cone said. "There's a trend in society — enlarge the honor roll. Basketball reflects society. I wouldn't want to be told that just because I came from a little school I couldn't compete for a job at a big school. And I don't think it's fair to tell the kids the same thing. There's too much stock put in championships. How many times have you heard it said, 'It's been 1954 since Milan'? I'm not so sure we need another Milan. So much of life is not dealing with a championship but with the path you take."

15

Stretch Drive

L YING in bed one night in January Hecklinski felt a pain in his right side near his liver. Or was it near the incision? He wasn't sure. "Pam," he said, "it hurts sleeping on my side." He'd felt strong coaching against Bloomington North ten days earlier.

The pain wasn't intense at first, but gradually it built. He thought maybe it was a pulled muscle. Maybe it would go away. He put off phoning Lexington — his next appointment wasn't until March 3. This was the first time he'd been allowed a long break between examinations. Pam agreed to let him put off the call because the numbers from his weekly liver tests taken in Anderson remained good. Besides, when he was active, especially during games, he didn't think about it.

He thought about it at night. That's when he'd go into Stephanie's room and kiss her good night, and come out and sit in his recliner in the den and remember his thoughts that helped him get out of the hospital after the surgery. "Yeah, man, I was afraid to die. I thought of myself, but I couldn't imagine, and I didn't want, Stephanie growing up without her father."

He hurt, but he kept coaching. It was important to him because Anderson's schedule was one of the toughest in the state and the toughest part was coming up next.

On a Tuesday night at Noblesville Hecklinski felt terrible. He coached all-out. The building was hot. Anderson won, 66–59, improving its record to 11–2. But Hecklinski felt so weak afterward that he could barely make it to some steps outside the locker room. Someone rushed to get him something to drink. After he'd cooled down, Pam drove him home. He wanted to be at his best that Saturday night when Ben Davis traveled to Anderson. Ben Davis had beaten Anderson in three straight regular-season games and had ended the Indians' season in the semistate at Hinkle the year before. A crowd of about 5,000 descended on the Wigwam on a night so frigid that people offered words of encouragement to the men directing traffic in the parking lot. Their heads were barely visible behind their breath.

Hecklinski still didn't feel well, but he had his players ready. He used the *Rocky III* movie script to motivate them — Rocky's manager was feeding the champ easy opponents. Hecklinski couldn't help his players in that way, he told them. This was defending champion Ben Davis they were playing. They would have to be aggressive and play their best, or lose.

Ben Davis, trailing throughout, rallied to go ahead for the first time late in the game. But typically, the Indians roused themselves, going on a 12–0 spurt to win, 64–56. Leaving the building, a few Anderson players heard the news that number one North Central had lost for the first time. A small cheer went up in the corridor outside the locker room. They had been climbing in the polls and were thinking of a number one ranking.

On Friday night, January 31, Anderson edged Kokomo by three

points at home as Bush led all scorers with 19. The next night at Carmel, north of Indianapolis, Anderson again won by three, but this time it took two overtimes. Bush stole the ball with four seconds remaining in the first overtime to preserve a tie, and stole the ball and scored a layup in the final 30 seconds of the second overtime for the victory. The Indians had won seven straight, and were now 15–2.

After the Carmel game, several players gathered at Bush's guardians' home. The Weatherfords lived in downtown Anderson, on Eighth Street, a picturesque road lined with Victorian houses. A birthday party was scheduled for one of the players, sophomore Derrick Jones. But twice police arrived on loud-noise complaints. Gary Weatherford objected to the officers' behavior. "The police entered my house without probable cause and threatened me and my wife with arrest on a felony charge," he told reporters. "There was no drinking or smoking in the house." Weatherford filed a complaint with the Anderson Police Department, alleging harassment of him and Bush. Weatherford said he was prepared for whatever consequences resulted from the complaint because he believed he'd been wronged. The players were unsettled by the incident.

Hecklinski continued in pain. But the team kept winning. Another difficult game took Anderson upstate to Logansport. There, the Berries' Caleb Springer scored 28 of his team's first 39 points. But he managed only four in the fourth period after Bush — five ten to Springer's six four — joined Tyson Jones to double-team him. That was after Bush spoke up to Hecklinski: "Put me on him." Bush insured a four-point win with two free throws in the last 17 seconds. Anderson's record was 16–2, 4–0 in the North Central Conference. With that came Anderson's first number one ranking in the state in Hecklinski's tenure. The Associated Press poll put Anderson at the top. In the coaches' poll, number one went to Bloomington North, 16–1, the "1" having come at the Wigwam.

Hecklinski wouldn't give in to the pain, even though he'd said the first week of practice: "I'm not going to sacrifice my health for basketball." After the close victories, the Indians showed authority at home against Lawrence North of Indianapolis. They scored the game's last 12 points to win, 66–51. They went into their four-corners offense to clinch the victory. Whenever they went to the four corners they'd win, and Hecklinski reminded them that's what they always had to do: get ahead late and get into the four corners.

The schedule was going to get harder still. In three days New Castle would be coming to town with a 17–1 record. New Castle had two six-foot-eight players and good outside shooting. This was February, when the majority of high school coaches in Indiana begin to look ahead and try to fine-tune their teams for the postseason. But teams such as Anderson and New Castle had to keep battling in important games. Their meeting would decide the North Central Conference championship. And winning would be a matter of pride for both schools and their towns, only twenty miles apart.

The traffic in Anderson poked along past the yellow-block Lemon Drop Café, featuring hamburgers on toast, Anderson Glass & Mirror, and Anderson Transmission & Clutches. Almost 3,000 fans were on the way from New Castle and more than that from around town. Parking spaces in the lots near the Wigwam filled early. Tournament time loomed, but this Friday night, February 14, had the feel of a postseason already arrived. Number one Anderson versus fourth-ranked New Castle. New Castle fans overflowed the abundant end zone seating, while the red-and-green-clad home faithful occupied both sides of the court. What they got was pure intensity.

Hecklinski shot off the bench to argue a foul call. "Go get 'im, Heck," somebody shouted.

"Did the bus pick you up at New Castle?" a woman from Anderson yelled at an official who called a fourth foul on Eric Bush. Anderson was leading 38–34, but now Bush had to be careful because almost eleven minutes remained in the game.

The score was tied at 42 after three quarters. As loud as the cheering got during that break in the action, the whistle of a freight slowly passing the front door could be heard, however slightly.

New Castle took the lead opening the fourth period, and clung to it despite an impressive offensive effort by Bush. He scored a three-pointer to close the margin to 51–50 with four minutes to go. He hit another three to close it to 58–57 with two minutes left. He stole the ball and fed it to Tyson Jones to leave Anderson behind 62–59 with one minute left. He hit a short jumper to close it to 63–61 with 45 seconds left. But trying desperately to get the ball back with 24 seconds left and New Castle leading, 64–61, Bush fouled out. Final: 67–61, New Castle. Its fans rushed onto the floor to celebrate; Hecklinski and his players picked their way through the mob.

In Hecklinski's view, Anderson lost the game early when its players failed to concentrate after some foul calls they questioned. "I almost killed the ref," Hecklinski fumed at his office desk, showing no sign of pain — he was too angry to feel it.

"He made that one call. I said, 'Jesus Christ, Dan . . .' He comes back and says, 'Don't you talk about my Lord like that.' I should have said, 'Hey, I'm with the Lord as much as anybody.' "

Hecklinski said his players should have let him worry about the officiating. Instead, they shot only six for 31 in the first half. "The number one ranking, all the bullshit, that doesn't matter to me," he said. "I'm not pissed because I'm not number one. I'm pissed because we didn't handle adversity."

He held his head and tried to rationalize, talking as much to himself as his glum assistants.

"You're not dealing with pros, man. You're dealing with high school kids, and you've got to try to guide 'em and try to lead 'em. But there's no excuse for not keeping your head in the game. There's no excuse for that. None. Eighth graders should keep their heads in the game.

"I hope they can get themselves back together. They have before. When they were freshmen they lost to North Central by twenty-five in the last game of the season and beat favorite Highland in the first game of the sectional. Played well. This season we were eight and one and lost our tenth game and rattled off nine wins in a row — should have been ten. It's hard to stay focused for a long, long time. I saw it in our pregame warm-up. I could tell in the locker room. That's why I have respect for great teams. They have a special quality, to remain focused, to keep doing it. I don't think we're a great team.

"John" — turning to Wilson — "you need to spend some time with Bush on that stuff" — he meant remaining unruffled despite such distractions as officials' calls — "because I'll just go off. I lose my patience. On Monday you take him and you watch the film with him."

Hecklinski looked down the final statistics sheet, banging the table at one player's output. "Nothing. Nothing. . . ."

"If we went out there and just played our guts out, if we lose the game and just really compete and get after it, that's cool. But I'm upset over how we lost it. I term it a loss because of a poor attitude in that game. It wasn't because they beat us."

Had the number one ranking distracted them?

"Didn't hurt us against Lawrence North."

Assistant Terry Turner said, "And you know what's crazy? Lawrence North is better than that team."

Hecklinski added, "Yeah, they are. Yeah, they are. We just didn't play tonight."

Hecklinski mulled the realities for forty-five minutes until, with almost everyone gone, he walked out of his office to greet some friends waiting with his wife. In the hall leading to the court he came to a full stop and turned. He dipped his head slightly. "I just hate to lose," he said, each word coming slowly. "I just hate to lose."

Anderson's game at Muncie Central was reminiscent of the Noblesville game. Both had been rescheduled because of snow. Hecklinski felt ill again.

He still was discouraged by the loss to New Castle. Anderson hadn't lost two straight games all season, and he didn't want another setback with the tournament just a week away. He had been thinking about these things before he even got to Muncie. During the game he got so overwrought he had trouble walking from the court after Anderson barely hung on to win, 60–59. The team had not played well, almost as if it already had peaked.

Though his strength was sapped, he held a thirty-minute closed-door meeting with the players. He told them they weren't playing as a team, and some weren't accepting blame for mistakes. By the time Pam had driven him home he felt as exhausted as he had early in the season. It was late. She went off to bed. He went to the den. It was quiet. Now he felt the pain in his stomach. He took out a Bob Seger CD, sat in his recliner, and began to replay the game in his mind. Then the music intruded.

"Against the wind, we were runnin' against the wind . . ."

He thought: His whole life he'd been running against the wind. Just like the song. It didn't seem that long ago when things were fine, and then the years passed and trouble came. The difference from the song was, of course, he wasn't alone. He had Pam. And Stephanie. He sat, hurting physically, but the more he thought the better he felt, in his mind. In Bob Seger, he hadn't exactly plumbed Kant. But Hecklinski had been introspective enough to be onto something: "Everybody runs against the wind. We all do. That's what I'd done my whole life. But here's this uplifting moment for me, an important moment for me. We won but we didn't play particularly well. I'm thinking: 'Wouldn't it be something to have that feeling of running with the wind?' I said, 'I got that feeling. I've got it. God, it's good. I'm running with the wind, man. After all these years.' Right then. Right now. It's so much easier to run with the wind than against the wind. You can't explain it. You can't believe it."

He rushed upstairs to the bedroom. Pam was asleep.

"Pam, Pam, I've got something to tell you."

"What?" she said, awakening barely.

"I'm running with the wind, Pam. I'm running with the wind."

"Great. Great."

"No, it's true. It's really something. I'm running with the wind."

"Go to bed, Ron."

DeKalb, playing as had been expected before the season, took a 14–3 record to nearby Homestead for a Northeast Hoosier Conference game. Homestead — "the sleeping giant of our conference," according to DeKalb coach Cliff Hawkins — woke up late to erase a 15-point deficit. This was precisely the sort of game that a team with a dominant player should win, and naturally Luke Recker was asked to win it.

He had the game in his hands, one hand, then the other, dribbling out near midcourt with the final seconds ticking down and the score tied at 48. Recker had been dribbling since 1:24 remained on the clock. Homestead stayed back in a two-three zone. The scene looked like a freeze frame except for the bouncing ball. Recker knew exactly what he wanted to do, and with the clock showing six seconds he made his move. He drove to his left and leaped softly into the air. He rose up with perfect grace even though three Homestead players darted forward to contest the shot. He was above them when he released a 15-footer, and he was still aloft as the ball began its arc toward the basket and the defenders began descending.

Recker had been held to 14 points, but the ones that mattered most were about to be added. The ball swished through the net. Game to DeKalb.

The play verified why Recker had been ticketed to Indiana University for so long. It demonstrated, too, why DeKalb was on a seven-game winning streak and, as Hawkins said, why "the wheels didn't come off" his team at midseason.

Another play suggested that Recker had sufficient support among his teammates to make DeKalb a genuine contender for the state championship. DeKalb was playing on a Tuesday night, February 18, at Fort Wayne's Wayne High. The game was tied at 71 in the second overtime. DeKalb held the ball for almost two and a half minutes, then with 15 seconds remaining put its favorite play — "Indiana" — into motion. Of course Recker was involved. He was to get the ball on a screen play. But the entire Fort Wayne team shifted with him when he made a cut toward the right corner of the court. Easy decision, well made: Luke Barnett, the ball handler, flipped underneath the basket to the open six-ten Jan Thompson. Another game to DeKalb.

"We're playing awfully, awfully well," said Hawkins. DeKalb, 19–3, had beaten good teams, won close games, just about mastered the coach's trapping zone defense. Recker was playing like "Mr. Basketball."

"If you had a record of 18–1, were third in the coaches' poll and sixth in the AP poll, you'd say that coach was sitting on top of the world," said Merrillville's Jim East. "But at times I have not enjoyed this season. I've gone home and fretted and worried about things outside of basketball."

Example: It was after six o'clock on game night. Did East know where all his players were? Here came two straggling in late. They had a problem getting a ride. "Five years ago I may have . . ." East had a way of not completing sentences when his meaning was apparent. He settled down: "They heard from me. We got through it. We go on with life."

Example two: Player violates prominent team rule, grows chin whiskers. East is beside himself. What could the player be thinking? All East wants to do is draw X's and O's. But being a veteran coach, he's prepared for almost anything. He's got a razor and blades. What? The player has pimples on his chin and won't use a blade. East concedes — not on the whiskers, but the manner of their removal. Somewhere he's got an old electric razor. Where is it? Got it. The thing is so old it's going to yank the whiskers, hurt worse than a blade. That's the way the player wants it. He shaves. East shakes his head. "I'm having to monitor shaving routines."

Flip side of coaching for East: his three-guard offense was working better than he had expected. "I still like the power-up shot. Get the basket and maybe a foul. I still like the percentage play but . . ." His competitiveness was rising as the going got tougher. Coaches and media who were well removed downstate routinely voted Merrillville higher and higher in their weekly polls. Most knew nothing of Merrillville's ineligible reserves, player tardiness, and shaving crises. They voted on the basis of Merrillville's record and its history, and Jamaal Davis's presence. What next would befall East?

He had to wait no longer than Monday practice before a Friday night bus ride to LaPorte for a game with the three-point-shooting Slicers. Jovan Blacknell fell and struck his head. He couldn't remember much of anything until Wednesday, and could not practice until Thursday. By then Davis had the flu. No coach liked having his practice routine altered slightly, and East's entire week had gone awry. The coach told a man bound for LaPorte and the game, "I don't think you want to see this."

LaPorte was almost forty miles east of Merrillville, more than halfway to South Bend. The bus was on time. It was the game that was late. Vandals dropped silicon pellets onto the Slicers' court, leaving everything sticky and the junior varsity and varsity games delayed more than an hour while custodians, the LaPorte girls' team, and assorted bystanders cleaned the floor. East was so thoroughly off schedule he actually felt relaxed during the delay.

Of the week's strange events what happened next was hardest for East to believe: his team ran away to a 31–9 halftime lead, its best half of the season and LaPorte's worst. Merrillville won the second quarter 16–2. LaPorte finished the night converting only three of 25 three-point attempts. Using three guards by necessity, East had a tailor-made defense to cover LaPorte's three-point-shooting offense. "We're quick, we can get out and guard that three-point shot," he said. And there was Jamaal: "If they beat our quickness on the perimeter, we have the big guy." The big guy had blocked LaPorte's first three inside shots.

"Jamaal does intimidate," said East. He was almost day-dreaming. But he was entitled: Davis had been blocking six to eight shots a game over a three-week stretch. Merrillville rallied past Portage on the strength of three steals and baskets by Eugene Wilson. That gave Merrillville its third straight undefeated season in the Duneland Conference — serene sounding in name only. Carl Sandburg wrote of the peace and glories of the dunes, but the conference named for them featured rugged play, and most years it produced a team that went a good distance in the tournament.

"We're only giving up forty-eight points a game and other teams are shooting just thirty-six percent against us," said East. "If we have any success in the tournament it'll be because of our defense. If we have any success in the tournament . . ."

Batesville rolled on. Around the state, the only question about Batesville was the caliber of its opponents. But every time Batesville played a bigger school it won, or was close. In Siefert's four seasons, Batesville never had been blown out of a game; the rare defeats always were excruciatingly close. Menser had the ability never to let a game get away from his team. If the Bulldogs hadn't lost, 41–40, at Kokomo they would be undefeated and ranked first in the state. As it was, they were number three. New Castle, by beating Anderson, had become number one among the media (Bloomington North was ranked first by the coaches). New Castle appeared the likely showdown opponent for Batesville in the tournament regionals at New Castle in what would be a tournament rematch from the previous season, when New Castle prevailed by a single point.

Batesville's record went to 18–1 at Lawrenceburg, bringing up a tricky Eastern Indiana Athletic Conference game at Franklin County in the town of Brookville. Franklin County had been the last team before Kokomo to beat Batesville in a regular-season game, breaking a fifteen-game Batesville winning streak in 1995–96 with a three-point overtime victory. But this time Menser scored 30, including nine of the final 11 points of the third period, in a 65–44 victory. Siefert removed him with 6:21 to play. Franklin County's Jim Pugh appreciated the kindness. Pugh admired Menser. "He's the best high school basketball player I've coached — I had the opportunity to coach him in AAU," Pugh said. "And he's the best high school player I ever coached against."

Batesville won easily at North Decatur and at South Decatur, both located in Greensburg. Menser scored 45 points total in limited action in the two games. After another Batesville victory, Rushville coach Jerry Craig put his arm around Menser's shoulder and told him: "Next to your parents and your coach, I'm your biggest fan."

"Thanks, Coach, I appreciate that."

Batesville would finish the regular season with a 22–1 record, best in the state. In southeastern Indiana, people's minds drifted to another time and another place — to 1954, to Milan.

16

The Last Draw

T 11 A.M. on Sunday, February 16, 1997, Indianans
turned on their televisions to watch the traditional draw
for tournament play. Finding out which team would
play which was an annual rite that even cut into church
attendance. This draw would be the last under the one-
class system. Before the telecast, Indiana Athletic Association
commissioner Bob Gardner plucked Ping-Pong balls out of a
hopper to determine the matchups so that WNDY-TV workers
could post them in advance to keep the program to an hour. Even
Gardner, advocate of change, couldn't overlook the sentiment
attached to this draw. "I used to listen to it on the radio and I had
my pencil ready," he said.

The 382 teams, each hoping to avoid a single loss and elimination, were grouped into 64 sectionals, to be played at such
sites as Anderson, Bedford, Ben Davis, Boonville, Brownsburg. . . .

Sixty-four teams would have home-court advantage, awarded because of the size of their gyms. Most sectional play was scheduled to begin Tuesday night, February 25, and continue on Thursday and Friday nights. Some teams would have to win three games to advance to regional play, others would get a first-game "bye" and have to win only two. Typically, six teams were grouped in a sectional. Four would play in a Tuesday doubleheader with two passing directly to the semifinals on Thursday by virtue of drawing a coveted "bye" game.

The 64 sectional winners advanced to regionals held at 16 sites on Saturday, March 8. Those 16 winners moved on to four semistates on Saturday, March 15, at Hinkle Fieldhouse in Indianapolis, Roberts Stadium in Evansville, Mackey Arena on the Purdue campus in West Lafayette, and the Fort Wayne Coliseum — with the final four playing off on Saturday, March 22, at the RCA Dome in Indianapolis. The idea that a team would have to win twice a day on the three consecutive Saturdays of the regionals, semistates, and finals to be the last team left — the champion — heightened fan fervor with the promise of drama. But more, the hurdles underscored how much the tournament had to be treated as a learning experience in how to cope with setback, take satisfaction in striving.

Anderson, 19–3, drew a "bye" and was favored to win its sectional in two games.

DeKalb, 20–3, also would be a host in the sectional round. It would have to win three games but, like Anderson, was a prohibitive favorite. No team in DeKalb's sectional had a player to match Recker.

Merrillville, 18–2, had its sectional at home as well. But it had lost its last regular-season game, to East Chicago Central, after which Jim East dropped one of his starters from the roster for violating team rules. Often, East expounded on the miseries of coaching. But going into the tournament he sounded more determined than at any time during his troublesome season. "We

played with three guards, we'll play with four — and Jamaal,"
he said.

Davis had played well against East Chicago Central, but not before raising concern again about his health. He had had the fainting
spell before the season. The morning of the East Chicago Central
game he woke up with chest pains. Again he was examined by
doctors. The pains subsided, nothing wrong could be found, and
he was cleared to play. East said that doctors attributed both the
fainting and the chest pains to "anxiety."

Batesville did not have an ideal sectional. The site was Greensburg, not Batesville. Batesville would have to win three games. In
all likelihood it would have to beat two teams for a third time
during the season; winning three times against any team is difficult, and the consolidated school Jac-Cen-Del was good, its only
two losses having come against Batesville. The home team,
Greensburg, also was capable.

In Indianapolis, attention centered on two teams: Ben Davis,
which would be trying to equal Franklin (1920–22) and Marion
(1985–87) as the only schools to win three straight state championships, and North Central, whose swift guard Jason Gardner
had proven to be the best sophomore in Indiana. And North
Central had Huggy Dye. Ben Davis had closed its regular season
with seven straight victories for a 16–4 record; North Central had
been beaten in three close road games to end 19–3. Still, a third
Ben Davis–North Central matchup seemed likely for the regional
final at Hinkle Fieldhouse.

Meanwhile, action — or inaction — by the state legislature
made it all but official that this would be Indiana's last single-
class tournament. The bill that would have allowed the nonbinding
referendum on the issue, thus delaying the switch to four classes
of basketball, went nowhere in the House committee. The legislation died with a 3–3 committee vote, with two committee members not present.

The tie meant that the bill could be brought up again, but committee chairman Thomas Alevizos, while having voted for the bill, said he would not allow another vote. "That's enough," he said. "I think we've devoted enough time to this."

Plump was in the room. He shook hands amiably with those on both sides of the issue. Lawrence Buell, a representative from Indianapolis who had submitted the bill, promised Plump he would keep up the fight. Plump took it as a kind remark, without hope.

He walked slowly from the building to a parking garage across the street, got his car, and drove to his restaurant, Plump's Last Shot. It was an old wooden neighborhood house, refurbished. Milan memorabilia gave it the feel of Milan itself rather than uptown Indianapolis.

It was quiet in there on a Thursday afternoon, another cold, gray February day. Plump sat in a corner of the front room. He looked beaten. As the most outspoken critic of class basketball he'd heard criticisms that he was a publicity seeker and even that he still "slept in his uniform."

"The thing that hurts the most," he said softly, "is that kids won't have the chance to experience what we did."

17

The Tournament

The cornerstone of the high school game has always been the one-class tournament. The best argument in its favor is not that it gives the smallest schools the chance to win it all, but that it gives them the chance to compete. No Indiana high school basketball player or team has ever ended a season and thought wistfully, "I wonder how good we really are? I wonder if we could compete against the best?"
• RON NEWLIN, *former executive director of the Indiana Basketball Hall of Fame*

There are an awful lot of teams that have outstanding players, that put together excellent regular seasons. But by the time our state tournament comes around I think you have to have a group that somehow just doesn't really want to die. Each year a team dies when you lose a game in the tournament and you're no longer a team. Well, if you can get that togetherness to the point where they're just not willing to die, I think that maybe that's what puts you over the top.
• AL RHODES, *coach of Warsaw, state champions, 1984*

> For broken dreams the cure is,
> Dream again
> And deeper . . .
> • C. S. LEWIS

ON TUESDAY evening, February 25, 1997, Indiana began its eighty-seventh and last single-class high school basketball tournament.

U.S. 231 leads straight south to Huntingburg and the best attended of all 64 sectionals that begin the annual single-class tournament. Less than an hour before the opening tip, static on the car radio dissolved and voices came clear. The talk was about the games in Huntingburg.

It sounded like a coach: "It's going to be a tough game and we're anticipating that. It's just tradition. Teams come in there and surprise you, a team that may not have had a great season will come in there and get a big win. Everybody in there's tough. . . ."

No team really was that tough, only one having been ranked in the top twenty during the season. But people flocked to Huntingburg anyway. That was a beauty, and mystery, of the event known since 1972–73 as the Southridge sectional, following the merger of Huntingburg and Holland high schools into Southridge High. The Pike Central Chargers were the rated team. The others were the Jasper Wildcats, the Southridge Raiders, the Northeast Dubois (pronounced either "Du-boys" or "Du-boice") Jeeps, the Forest Park Rangers, and the Wood Memorial Trojans. "People come because it means bragging rights," said Jasper athletic director Denny Lewis. "Everybody works in the same places, so the winners can rub it in for a whole year."

The sectional had never failed to sell out — 6,200 a night for three nights — since 1952, a year after the building went up. Even school consolidation from the late fifties through the early seventies couldn't dampen the annual celebration. Vanished were high schools in Birdseye, Ferdinand, French Lick, Ireland (its school teams had been known as the Spuds), Otwell, Spurgeon, West Baden, and Winslow; Birdseye used to turn out practically the entire town for the sectional. Other teams took their places. If anything, it was harder this season than any other to get a seat because an era was ending.

The six schools in Huntingburg would be playing in three different classes the next year. But despite the varying sizes of the schools, none had ever dominated the single-class sectional. That was part of its charm. Anyone could win, and quite often the winner was a surprise.

"Because they bring together teams from neighboring communities, sectionals create a competitive zeal among teams and fans that isn't equaled at later stages of the tournament," basketball authority Jack Schneider wrote in the *Herald* of Jasper.

"Everybody gets 'up' for this sectional," said Jasper's Lewis. "The teams. The fans. You go into the Huntingburg gym for a game on a February night, come out of that tunnel, everybody's screaming, it's like a hundred degrees — and those people act like they don't even know you. The tournament's even more exciting."

The *Huntingburg Press* carried an account by J. A. Dotterweich that began: "My earliest recollection of the local sectional is sitting in the kitchen of our rural Huntingburg home on Route 3 with my feet propped up in front of our old wood-burning cookstove, listening intently to a play-by-play broadcast coming over our family's vacuum tube mono RCA Victor radio in a cabinet about the size of a small three-drawer dresser."

A radio voice, at fever pitch: "Wildcat basketball is on the air tonight as the opening round of the Southridge sectional gets under way as the Jeeps of Northeast Dubois take on the W-i-i-l-l-ld-cats of Jasper. . . ." A sign in Jasper: "GO WILDCATS." A boy shot baskets in his driveway almost in the shadow of a water tower inscribed "CITY OF JASPER." The WITZ-FM play-by-play man, from the gym: "Good evening, everyone, from the Huntingburg Memorial Gymnasium. . . . It's going to be a dandy county rivalry . . ." He shouted above the noise.

Almost everyone who was coming was in the gym; the parking lot had but a space or two left. The crowd noise still was blaring from the car radio but blasting even louder out of the building's open doors, creating a stereo effect. Because the court was in a sunken bowl, the structure did not appear imposing, simply a one-story brick building on Route 231, Main Street, between Fifth and Sixth. But inside was solid humanity, people standing. The happy smell of buttered popcorn hung in the air. The court glistened below, a bright rectangle seen through a faint haze, as if the dust of decades had been stirred.

Writers occupied high perches at the four corners. Benches were built on cast-iron legs and bolted to the concrete floor. It was now clear what the radio play-by-play voice meant when he'd said he was about to describe a "bird's-eye view" of the games. Bleacher seats encircled the court and rose high up against the walls. Close to the top of one end, an inches-wide aisle enabled people to nudge from one side of the arena to the other. Among old photographs of players hanging on the walls between concession stands was a color portrait of William Menke, who'd been a star player for the old Huntingburg Happy Hunters. A Navy pilot, Menke had been killed during World War II. Nothing much about the gym had changed even as Larry Bird led Springs Valley to a sectional title in the mid-seventies and later Nick Nolte attended a sectional as part of his research for the film Blue Chips. The gym's office still was equipped with one dial phone, and you had to get an operator to connect to a town as close as Jasper.

The opening game was spirited and close, played between two teams with losing records during the regular season. The score was 9–6 at the quarter in favor of Northeast Dubois, and while there wasn't much scoring the crowd gave both teams a standing ovation after the first eight minutes. Dubois led 29–19 after three quarters before Jasper began a rally despite the cries of "Jeep, Jeep, Jeep . . ." It got so loud that Dubois coach Rob Haworth communicated to his players on the floor by using colored signs — yellow, green. With the score tied at 34 and only two minutes remaining, here came a yellow sign with some coded message, a black arrow pointed upward.

There was no sign available, however, to stop a five-foot-five substitute named Michael Denton. With the score still tied and only four seconds left, Denton took what may prove to be the shot of his life, certainly one to be talked about for some time in the barbershops of Jasper. It came flying out of the deep left corner and plopped through the net. Jasper, following a 6–14 regular season, had won, 37–34, and Denton was somewhere beneath a throng of players and fans.

"When you think of Indiana basketball you think of Luke Recker," said Jasper's coach, Ken Schultheis. "You don't think of a five-foot-five kid. But this sectional is the epitome of Hoosier Hysteria. This is the late 1990s, when nobody is supposed to be caring about high school athletics. I wish everyone in the country could experience the excitement in this gym. Doctors, politicians, everybody gets to be a kid again."

Schultheis also declared, "Mike Denton is Walter Mitty."

Denton had shot one for nine during the entire regular season.

Jasper history had repeated. In 1952 Junie Giesler sank a last-second shot to give the Wildcats a victory in the Vincennes Regional. Giesler stood five foot three. He played only eight seconds of the game. To this day he remains a big man in Jasper.

After a while, the Jasper players came out of their locker room to high-fives from people leaning out of the stands, and sat to watch the second game. After a longer while, the Northeast Dubois players emerged. They had on white shirts and ties, they had buzz haircuts, their eyes were red-rimmed. So were the eyes of the Dubois cheerleaders. Fans got out of their seats and moved toward the ends of the rows so they could reach out and pat the players on their backs as they climbed the steps at one corner of the building to be given sodas at a concession stand. Not one could manage a smile, not at that moment, not after those 32 minutes of furious play, not after having their season ended by the smallest kid on the court.

Unlike the fans at some postseason games, Huntingburg spectators stayed for the next game even if their team was beaten, and win or lose they returned for the second and third nights of the sectional. In the second game on opening night, Pike Central from Petersburg beat Forest Park, 48–30. Pike Central's Adam Seitz, a six-three-and-a-half junior guard and a Division I prospect, scored 26. On Thursday night he scored 21 as Pike Central ended Jasper's two-year streak as sectional champions, and the next night he added 16 as Pike Central beat Southridge to win the sectional. At the end, Southridge coach Ray Roesner said: "Realistically, we knew when we bounced the first ball out there who the favorite was going to be. All we wanted was a chance. We got that chance and we didn't do it. I would have loved to have won this since it was the last one, but Pike Central was very deserving."

Ben Davis was favored to win its sixth straight sectional and more — tournament talk almost always included the school that was coming off two straight state titles and an unprecedented four straight final-four appearances. The road to the dome in downtown Indianapolis was only twelve miles or so from the school on the west side of the city, and that included stops for both the regionals and semistates at Butler's Hinkle Fieldhouse. Ben Davis was a natural pick for the final four because Steve Witty's teams had won 22 of 25 games at Hinkle since 1990, including 16 straight in the postseason dating from 1993. "We think of Hinkle as our home away from home," Witty said.

For its sectional Ben Davis drew a bye, then for its Thursday game faced Pike — not downstate Pike Central but Indianapolis Pike, which during the regular season had split two games with Ben Davis and stopped North Central's streak after its 14–0 start. John McCarroll, a surgeon whose practice included Ben Davis players, arrived early for the game and chatted with Pete Saunders, a Ben Davis booster. Before long their conversation turned to a famous Ben Davis game, in the 1995 regional at Hinkle, against Indianapolis Washington, alma mater of favorite Indy son George McGinnis. Fans had lined up hours early to get in, and weren't disappointed. It had been dubbed "the last great high school basketball game," and from all accounts it wasn't hyperbole.

"They're running up and down the court, it's just magnificent, and we're all cheering, we're not even arguing, we don't even care who wins," McCarroll said. "Fifteen thousand packed in there to see this game. What was great was, here were about ten guys seated together, none of us knew each other and basketball was our common thread. Basketball brought us together."

"Hinkle is high school ball at its best," said Saunders.

It was back and forth between Ben Davis and Washington until Washington took a 77–76 lead on two free throws with four seconds left. The inbounds pass went to Ahmed Bellamy because that year's "Mr. Basketball," Damon Frierson, was covered. Two Washington defenders chased Bellamy away from the basket after he'd crossed midcourt, so that he was going in the wrong direction when he launched a 22-footer on the run. Nothing but net. End of game. And that was the last basketball game played by Indianapolis Washington, which closed that year. McGinnis was there, and he cried. A big man hurting. "It was probably one of the great games — it was everything you could want from a high school basketball game," he said. "It was tough to lose. But it was much tougher to me because the school was closing."

The 1997 Ben Davis team seemed much like the 1996 champions, who had lost six times before the tournament. Both teams were well drilled in fundamentals and well conditioned. Witty's practices were practically clinics in time management — not a moment was wasted. Near the end of one session, Witty worked his players into a lather with a fandango that included sprinting the length of the floor several times, high-speed push-ups, back-pedaling with hands up, stepping in place, and defending imaginary ball handlers. Like an orchestra conductor, an assistant coach directed the finishing flourish to each repetition, motioning some players to peel off in one direction, others in another. "It's the 'Cincy Shuffle,'" said Witty. "It's good for stance, footwork, and conditioning. I got it from the University of Cincinnati in the seventies."

Ben Davis, ranked sixth by the coaches, finished strong against Pike with a 22–6 fourth quarter and won, 52–45. The next night Ben Davis beat Brebeuf and headed toward Hinkle and, apparently, another game against North Central. But first North Central, which also won its sectional, and Ben Davis had to win their games in the doubleheader to open the regional. Then they would meet that same night for the regional championship. The consensus was that the Hinkle "home" floor would be enough to give Ben Davis the advantage over North Central a third time around.

A man wearing a brown "Charlie Daniels Band" cap seated at the counter at Frisch's Big Boy in Greensburg was finishing his pie and talking about having been at the Connersville sectional the night before and saying that now he was heading to the high school gym for the Batesville-Greensburg sectional championship, and what a crowd there would be because the two teams had won the previous night's doubleheader by a combined three points, and that he would be happy to lead the two visitors there except that they were only on their main course and he didn't want to get shut out at the door. And so he said good-bye.

The evening before, Batesville barely had scored a third victory over Jac-Cen-Del, which finished its season at 18–3. With only 297 students, Jac-Cen-Del was a small-school team that Batesville's Melvin Siefert said "should be ranked if we're the number three team." The games had been so hard fought and tense that, according to the *Greensburg Daily News*, the Decatur County Council meeting to formalize a plan to brick the outside of the courthouse had been repeatedly interrupted so that members could get updates on the scores from radio.

The Greensburg gym had been jammed and would be again for the Batesville-Greensburg final. Traffic wound through the town's streets. Cars were parked on the sides of the roads. People hurried inside, under the scrutiny of Greensburg's athletic director Dave Jarvis, six foot seven. Everyone was orderly, although keyed up by the long-standing rivalry. Some already were cheering. A boy painting his face in front of a men's-room mirror said that he was for Greensburg and that it was a G taking shape in blue on his cheek.

Fran Telles, sixty-eight, Batesville's beloved barber, made a rare appearance at the game. Almost every Thursday night at Telles's shop, Michael Menser cut teammate Matt Maple's hair and they all talked basketball. But Telles always said he couldn't close the shop in time to make the games and so he listened on radio. The real reason he stayed away from the games, according to Jenny Menser, was that Telles was afraid his heart would give out in the excitement. When he felt his heart beating faster as he listened at home he simply turned off the radio.

"This is horrible," exclaimed Telles, in the midst of the noise in the Greensburg gym. "You can't turn it off."

He survived — it was a pretty routine 64–54 victory for Batesville. But Jenny Menser said: "If he had seen the Jac-Cen-Del game he might have died."

Menser scored 25 points in the first half, 33 in all against Greensburg, and minutes before Batesville had run its record to 25–1, ten-year-old Ben Siefert, the coach's son, casually raised four fingers in the air — signifying Batesville's four straight sectional titles. Afterward, Greensburg coach Phil Snodgress greeted Menser out on the court and said, "You've got my vote for 'Mr. Basketball.'"

As a happy crowd swirled around him near midcourt, Siefert already was thinking ahead eight days to the regional at New Castle. It was almost certain now that Batesville would face another tournament showdown with New Castle in the regional. That week Siefert would call Jerry Craig, whose Rushville team had been beaten by New Castle as well as Batesville.

"Can we beat 'em?" Siefert asked.

"Yes," replied Craig. "And they can beat you."

Anderson, DeKalb, and Merrillville all won their sectionals to advance to the regionals.

Four small schools that would be placed the following year in Class 1A scored huge upsets to win sectionals. The smallest was Union, enrollment 134, located on the west side of the state in Dugger, set back fifteen miles off the main north-south road between Terre Haute and Vincennes. Barr-Reeve, enrollment 176, finished off its sectional by beating the host Washington Hatchets.

Several good teams were beaten. East Chicago Central lost its first sectional game, seeming to have nothing left after its double-overtime victory at Merrillville to end the regular season.

Milan, enrollment 349, lost out on its million-to-one (or more) chance to duplicate 1954 when it bowed 75–62 to Lawrenceburg in a sectional opener. During the season Milan had come from 14 points behind to beat Lawrenceburg on its court, the most memorable game of recent times for Milan. But Milan hadn't won a tournament game since 1989. After opening with a 6–3 record, the Indians were hurt by injuries and lost eight in a row, nine of their last ten, to begin the tournament with a 7–12 record.

Randy Combs addressed his team in the Milan gym, standing beneath the 1954 title banner, before the short bus ride to the South Dearborn gym in Aurora. The team stayed close in the game until a late 11–0 run by Lawrenceburg. After that, it was just a question of what Combs would tell his players when it was over. John Erardi of the *Cincinnati Enquirer* covered his remarks:

"Boys, you were competitive in every game. Every game we played in was a war. We fought. How many times did we get beat at the end of the ball game? How many? How many times did we face the face of adversity and come back? You reached down tonight, boys, and there was nothing left. You had used it all up.

"It doesn't even feel like the season is over. It went too fast. Sometimes, boys, life deals you things, and it doesn't seem like it's fair. But you go on. You gave me everything you had. With seven practices, you started your basketball season. And in ten days you had to play the third-ranked team in the state. You went from playing in the final-four football game to playing the third-ranked team in the state.

"Then, you don't get your break over Christmas, and you're down 19–5 and you come back to win after losing your leading scorer to injury. That's great character, boys. And then to have so many games go down to the wire the way they did the last couple of weeks. And to keep coming back and coming back, practicing hard, playing hard.

"It seems like we just got started. You made sacrifices on my behalf for what I had to do to try to get this basketball program headed in the right direction. I know this season isn't what you anticipated. But every day I knew I was going to get the absolute best effort you could give. And you gave it right until the very end. You set the example of what will be expected in the future."

On Monday, March 3, Ron Hecklinski finally went to Lexington for his medical appointment, and to confess that he had been in pain for six weeks.

"Doc, are you sure you didn't leave a sponge or some pliers in there?" he said to one of the doctors.

"If we left anything in, you'd be dead now," the doctor replied.

An examination revealed a hernia in the area of his incision. "I overdid it," Hecklinski admitted.

The doctor said he'd like to schedule the operation that Wednesday.

"This is regional week!" Hecklinski exclaimed. "I can't do it Wednesday."

One more time he forgot his words from the first week of practice: *"I'm not going to sacrifice my health for basketball."*

What if he phoned just as soon as his season was over?

Okay, the doctor said.

Hecklinski paused.

"How will I know," he asked, "if I've waited too long?"

"You won't be standing, asking the question."

18

The Regionals

EGIONAL Saturday in Indiana is like no other day. The basketball feast is sumptuous but so widespread that a person wishes he could be in four or five places at once. The heart tugs toward Batesville, the small-school hope. A plan is set. Follow Batesville to the New Castle regional. Should the Bulldogs lose their early game, Anderson in the Wigwam would beckon for its evening game. If somehow both Batesville and Anderson lost early, the prospect of North Central playing Ben Davis that evening at Hinkle would be next choice. Either that or Fort Wayne, where a thriller shaped up between Luke Recker's DeKalb and Cameron Stephens's Fort Wayne South Side. Then there was Merrillville, playing in Gary. As James Naismith discovered long ago watching high school basketball in Indiana, "The possibilities here are endless."

*   *   *

The sun had barely risen, but the waitresses in the Sherman House restaurant in Batesville were in full stride. "This won't be long because I know you boys are going to the game," said a woman taking a breakfast order. It was regional Saturday in Indiana, and practically everyone in Batesville was up early and ready to live and die this day with the Bulldogs. "GO BULLDOGS" signs were plastered through the town square and on the sweeping curved marquee of the art deco Gibson movie theater.

Before long, the team bus pulled up to the Sherman House, which looks like a German inn, reflecting the town's founders. All the players piled in for breakfast, which took only minutes because the cooks were ready for them. By nine o'clock the bus was back at school and lined up to lead a caravan of decorated cars, headlights on, north on Route 3 to New Castle for Batesville's 12:30 P.M. game with Connersville. If New Castle beat Winchester at 10:30 and Batesville won, the rematch from the previous year's regional would be on at 8 P.M. Almost half of Batesville was heading cross-country, but only because that's all the tickets the school had been allowed — just about everyone in Batesville wanted to be there.

All of Batesville would fill just more than half the 9,314 seats in the world's largest high school gym. But the three other participating schools had to be allotted their share. Batesville fans had sent an emissary to the ticket window at New Castle three times during the week; the first two times he returned with about 300 tickets but the third time he was turned away. When the first 1,411 tickets went on sale at the Batesville gym the previous Tuesday morning, people had been lined up since 2:30 A.M. Many sat it out in beach chairs, bundled in blankets.

Saturday morning's caravan of buses and cars stretched for more than a mile, but Jim Menser was almost a half hour ahead. He didn't like to poke along in caravans, and so he got an early start in the family Honda with Jenny in back and their daughter, Angie, up front. It was a crisp, brilliantly sunny morning. Jim looked serene with his eyes on the road that stretched out on the flat farmland. Two years earlier Angie had ranked first in her Batesville class, and Jenny said she would have liked it had Michael ranked in the top ten of his class of 127. "He's twelfth," she said, "but single digits sounds a lot better. . . . Hey, there's Jack Smith's van up there."

Almost everyone else was behind, including such Batesville regulars as Mae Ertel, eighty-one, grandmother of the Bulldogs' big man, six-foot-five Aaron Ertel — she watched games from a wheelchair; affable Velma Placke, who handed out Tootsie-Roll Pops at games to satisfy a superstition of hers; and Lowell Yorn, sixty-six, who'd missed only six games in twenty-seven years and closed his accounting business every March to watch the tournament. "The priorities," he said, "are family, church, and basketball."

People in Rushville, halfway to New Castle, had put up posters: "BEAT 'EM," and a small sign stuck into a front lawn, "J.D. WAS BORN HERE," meaning J. D. Vonderheide, a substitute on the Batesville team. Jim Menser was talking about Siefert's coaching abilities: "Melvin has a counseling degree" — a master's from Xavier University in Ohio. "He knows how to deal with players and still keep his discipline the way it has to be."

"Melvin called at 8:03 this morning. 'Is Mikey coming?'" said Jenny. "Three minutes late. I told him he was on the way."

She was more relaxed than Melvin, she said. Maybe it was just the beautiful early-March day. Writing that morning in Batesville's *Herald-Tribune*, Harlan Roberts warned in an editorial page column: "The weather is extremely mild and the Indiana high school boys' basketball sectional is history. Why do I mention the basketball sectional in the same breath as the weather? In the past, some of our worst winter weather has occurred the week of the basketball sectional. So, is winter over for us? My blooming crocuses say yes. The temperature is predicted to be in the low 70s today, another indication to say, yes, the winter is over. I say don't put away your snow shovel."

Jenny was carrying Imodium to New Castle, but the sectionals had been the more difficult time for her to the point that she said "each day I thought I was going to puke." She'd feared an upset loss. Her husband amplified: "The Greensburg tennis team beat us three years in a row and this year we beat them in tennis. We could just see it last week, them clicking us off in basketball."

Jenny's stomach was fine now, and after the early games, which went according to form — first New Castle won, and then Batesville followed, with Michael scoring 27 against Connersville — the Mensers went off to a smorgasbord in Hagerstown. Part of the ritual on the Saturdays of the regionals, semistates, and finals is filling in the hours between the end of the doubleheader and the beginning of the evening championship game. At least part of the time was devoted to gathering the results from other regionals, and the biggest early news of this day came from Hinkle Fieldhouse: Ben Davis had been upset in its morning game by Indianapolis Cathedral. To Batesville fans it was good news that the two-time defending champion would not be in their team's way if the Bulldogs could advance to the Hinkle semistate.

For the Batesville–New Castle game, people drove into New Castle during the afternoon from all around — a man from Chicago, a couple from Dayton. They expressed concern about getting tickets. Lines formed early at the doors, everyone soaking up the beauty of an early-evening sunlight that glowed orange. Somehow everyone got in for the encounter. An epic it would prove to be. Any basketball fan in the world who happened to perish in this next hour and a half would have been pleased to have died and gone to New Castle.

Almost an hour early, the place was filled with twin seas of green and blue, the two schools' colors. The Raintree Barbershop Chorus, Eugene Lacy, director, rendered "Moonlight on the Wabash" and "Back Home Again in Indiana."

I have always been a wand'rer,
Over land and sea,
Yet a moonbeam on the water
Casts a spell o'er me.
A vision fair I see
Again I seem to be:
Back home again
In Indiana,
And it seems that I can see
The gleaming candlelight still shining bright
Thru the sycamores for me . . .

There were almost 10,000 people in the building and it sounded like none during those songs that affirmed everything it meant to be a Hoosier. Reverential silence was kept to the very last note. Dry eyes were few.

And then they played basketball — 23–1 New Castle, top-ranked by the media, and 26–1 Batesville, number three. The *Indianapolis Star* the next morning headlined it as a game "for the ages."

Menser finished off the first quarter with a 30-footer at the buzzer to give Batesville a 16–8 lead. It was 23–17 Batesville at the half. In the third period a guard for New Castle named Skipper Rowland asserted himself with two three-pointers, and New Castle moved ahead. Menser kept the New Castle lead at just 37–36 after three periods with another buzzer-beating three-pointer. The shot was remarkable. Double-teamed, he was moving to his left when he stopped, then in one motion elevated and made a one-quarter turn to his right before releasing the ball. It was a stirring and transcendent moment produced by a kid twelfth in his class and without ego. It was a shot he had practiced until he did it just the way Oscar Robertson once described making a big play in a big game: "It's like a ballet. It's like a dance that you do. You do things without even thinking about them."

But New Castle's twin six-foot-eight towers took a toll on Aaron

Ertel, who picked up his fourth foul with seven and a half minutes left and had to sit down. New Castle opened up a 41–36 advantage. Menser pulled off a tie at 44 by leaping high above a close-guarding defender for a three-pointer with three and a half minutes to go. But Ertel fouled out with 47 seconds left, New Castle added a point for a 47–45 lead, and that left it up to Menser.

Menser dribbled away the clock — while Batesville was trailing. Siefert had that much confidence that Menser would tie the game or win it at the end.

With five seconds remaining, he drove inside, swept along the baseline, his body low, his head bobbing no higher than the waistbands of the tall defenders. He was fouled. He'd shoot one and one. The noise level was now the opposite of what it had been for the barbershop singers. It was bedlam. Menser stood there and calmly sank two free throws, forcing overtime.

And he did it again with 34 seconds left in overtime, converting a one-and-one situation for a one-point Batesville lead, 58–57. Big Joey Gaw hit a put-back shot with 15 seconds remaining to put New Castle up by one. It was reminiscent of Kokomo's shot that had given Batesville its only loss. And so again it was up to Menser. And New Castle was determined not to let him win the game.

As he crossed the midcourt line with New Castle leading, 59–58, three — three! — New Castle players jumped out on him, surrounding him. Nevertheless, Menser gave Batesville a chance to win. From deep trouble near the right sideline, he executed a deft pass, a ticket to the semistates. The ball went to a teammate who was open for a 15-footer just to the left of the key. He took one step forward. He hesitated. He was in that "in between" area where the shot looks simpler than it is, where a shooter sometimes can find it hard to pull the trigger. But the thought flashed across the minds of Batesville rooters: make it or miss it, just take it. But he didn't. He looked away from the basket and passed the ball underneath, and that teammate was well guarded. The ball caromed off the Batesville player's leg and out of bounds. That was it. Menser fouled out with two seconds left, Gaw added two free throws. The final was 61–58, New Castle.

Columnist Bill Benner of the *Indianapolis Star* had taken in three basketball games — pro, college, and high school — in 25 hours. He'd seen the Chicago Bulls, "the best basketball team on the planet"; a crucial Big Ten game at Purdue; and the Batesville–New Castle regional championship. "For the first time in my sportswriting career, I had to wipe tears from my eyes before I could cover a ball game," he wrote, referring to the Raintree Barbershop Chorus. And: "What transpired was a game too wonderful for mere words. Yes, the bigger school won. But it wasn't because New Castle was bigger. It's because it was better by an incredibly thin margin. . . . Of the three games I saw in the last 25 hours, this was the best by far. And certainly the only one that made me cry."

In the Batesville locker room no one spoke. Someone opened a door nearby and the squeak sounded like thunder. The players, Menser in the middle, sat and waited for Siefert. Menser stared at the floor as did most of the others. Two cried. Siefert's son sobbed near the door. Siefert's eyes filled with tears as he walked across the room slowly and stood in front of the players. He had a hard time starting to speak and his voice caught and stuck several times, so that it took a while for him to say, "They can take all the trophies they want. That's fine. But I'm proud of you guys. Several times there you could have rolled over and died and you didn't. To the seniors, I want to thank you for four great years. I couldn't have gotten any more out of you than what you gave me. You played your hearts out every time out this year, every time. Now we have to turn the page, move on. Different things. New careers, new goals. You younger guys, get ready for next year." He paused. "One, two, three . . ." And they all chanted, "Bulldogs."

Siefert then sat on a bench, his arm around his son's shoulders.

When they met the massed media, Menser looked in better shape than Siefert. The coach sat, with red eyes and tie undone, on the floor of an auxiliary gym, his back against folded bleachers.

He told how difficult it was for him because he'd begun as head coach four years before with this group of seniors. A more composed Menser sat on a chair and answered questions at length. He had scored 22 points and averaged 24.9 for the season. He said he'd be going to play in college and was most concerned at the moment about his senior teammates who wouldn't be playing organized basketball anymore.

But: "I guarantee you, personally, when I look back on this, I'd rather — much rather — go out this way than have class basketball. Because that's what Hoosier Hysteria is all about. It's not about being better than every school the same size that you are, it's about beating anybody in the state. I think they're killing it."

Anderson, having finished its season ranked fifth in the state by the AP, faced a difficult game at 12:30 P.M. in the Wigwam against number six Muncie South. But the Indians played one of their best games of the season and won, 76–66. Hecklinski called the up-tempo contest "one of the best games in the state all year. It was much better than our games against Ben Davis, DeKalb, Bloomington North — it topped them all. Muncie South was so quick and we were, too. Every play was big."

But a stunning side event occurred. During the fourth quarter, Anderson police entered the building and arrested Gary Weatherford on a misdemeanor charge of contributing to the delinquency of a minor. The warrant for his arrest stemmed from the incident at the Weatherfords' home when he was giving the birthday party for Derrick Jones more than a month earlier. Weatherford was approached at his seat and escorted to a corridor in the Wigwam, where he was handcuffed, then taken away in a patrol car.

Bush saw his guardian being led away and could barely believe the rest of the story when he was told it. It wasn't long after that that he came down with an upset stomach. As pressure filled as all the games he'd played before had been, he'd never gotten an

207

upset stomach. Hecklinski tried to keep Bush calm. "You'll have to play through this thing," Hecklinski told him. Eric responded quietly that he was "all right with it." But he wasn't; he literally was sick over Weatherford's arrest.

Two days later, Anderson's assistant police chief would tell reporters that the timing of the arrest was botched and that the department would conduct an internal investigation. The assistant chief, named Ron Crouse, was quoted by the *Herald Bulletin* of Anderson: "We think there was a communication breakdown in the department that led to the issuance of a warrant" — that is, a warrant instead of a summons. "Even if there was a warrant on file, could this situation have been handled more appropriately? Appearance is that this could have been handled better. I can't defend it."

Cindy Weatherford posted $2,000 bond and Gary was back with her in their seats for the night game. But "it definitely affected Eric," said Gary.

Anderson's opponent was Delta, a surprise to have advanced so far in the tournament. Even some Hoosiers weren't sure where Delta was — only twenty miles up the road from Anderson, five miles north of Muncie on land where city and country merged. Delta not only had been unranked, it had shown no sign — no early sign, anyway — of a successful season. It got off to a 3–3 record, and lost by 27 points to Muncie South and lost even to little Wapahani, where Hecklinski had begun his coaching career.

But Delta had improved vastly after its loss to Wapahani. Paul Keller, Delta's forty-one-year-old coach, began to emphasize defense and played to win relatively low-scoring games. With that, Delta won 18 of its next 19, and its fans wondered if the impossible dream might be theirs. Could Delta become the first school with fewer than a thousand students — it had 916 — to win the state title since Plymouth in 1982?

Delta had long been overshadowed by nearby schools — especially by Muncie Central, with its eight state championships, and the highly ranked Muncie South. But now against Anderson, Delta applied plenty of defense, stopping the Indians without a field goal in the second quarter. Suddenly Anderson partisans in the Wigwam were wondering about, worried about Delta.

It was a standing-room-only crowd, and it was seeing a shocker: Delta making a 12–0 run to take a 20–17 lead midway in the second quarter, hanging on to a 31–23 lead midway through the third quarter. Anderson looked sluggish. But then the Indians rallied, increasing their own defensive pressure and forcing three turnovers that led to easy baskets to cut Delta's lead to 31–30.

But Patrick Jackson, a Delta junior guard, played brilliantly. He scored 25 points, including the first seven of the fourth period and 15 in that decisive final quarter. Anderson simply had nothing left as Delta scored 24 fourth-quarter points to break a tie after three periods. Unranked Delta won, 56–48, to end Anderson's 21-game regional victory streak in the Wigwam.

Bush scored only nine points. He scored only nine against Muncie South, but had played well in directing the team from the point. At night he looked tired. Hecklinski didn't want to use the arrest as an excuse. "I think it was more a case of Eric having given everything he had in the first game. That's how he plays — he gives everything." For the season, Bush averaged 14.8 points and 4.8 assists. But it was Delta headed for Hinkle Fieldhouse and a semistate appearance for the first time in its 30-year history.

Hecklinski said that Anderson showed both fatigue and a lack of disciplined play in the fourth period. They had weakened during fourth periods against North Central, Bloomington North, New Castle, and Muncie South, all powerful teams, but still had managed victories against Bloomington North and Muncie South. The Anderson players needed to work more on weight training and to play smarter the following season when most would be seniors.

Like all good Indiana teams, Delta had good guards. Its point man, Billy Lynch, seldom scored — he didn't score a point against

Anderson. But he slowed Bush and didn't turn the ball over. Jackson, the other guard, told reporters, "This being the last year of one-class basketball, we came here wanting to make a statement. We're a small school and Anderson is a tradition-rich team ranked fifth in the state. We wanted to make a final statement that small schools can play in big gyms."

Hecklinski had feared the second game immediately after getting past the first one. It was a natural feeling for a coach, but it had been warranted because his players had been run ragged by Muncie South. "That game didn't get over until almost two o'clock, so I knew going into the eight o'clock game we were going to be fatigued," he said. "I knew it, and we were. Both physically and mentally. It's natural for kids. Delta, a very, very good team, didn't have to play a very difficult morning game. They got two or three more hours of rest. So it was a situation where I knew it was going to be tough no matter how good Delta was or how good they weren't. And they are pretty good."

Once more, Hecklinski's emotions and his reason collided following the season-ending loss. The coach was angry and stayed that way for at least half of a fifteen-minute locker-room speech to his players.

"I was mad," he recalled, "because at the end of three quarters the score was tied. Whoever could sustain their play for eight minutes would win the game. And we didn't. They got the first couple of points in the fourth quarter, so we never were able to get into our four-corner offense, which is very difficult for teams to play against. We could never get to that point because we were never ahead. We made some plays down the stretch that weren't very good plays. But they were plays that were very characteristic of a tired team. And so I came into the locker room very upset, very loud.

"But as I went on I just had an understanding of what actually happened and I calmed myself down. Nobody intentionally missed any shots or intentionally screwed up — they were tired. I said,

'Hey, that's just the way it is. You've got to take the good with the bad. You had a great run. You ended up 22–4.' Aaron Boyd was a starter for four years; I thanked him for being a big part of our program and being a big part of me for four years. I thanked them all for helping me recover because, as I told them, after I'd come out of surgery and I was going through the tough times the one thing that got me through was knowing that I was going to coach my team again. I said, 'Knowing that and having that to hang on to, to look forward to, to dream about, being able to coach, was what really got me through. Thanks for being there for me. And I hope I've been there for you.' "

He felt sad as he walked out of the room. "As a coach," he said, "I dread that last game because I dread to see my players crying." But Pam was there. "We've already won our 'state championship,' " she told him.

Delta's Coach Keller had seen a number of games in the Wigwam and loved the place as much as the Indians and their followers. He called it "the mecca of Indiana basketball" — without question it was one of those spiritually soothing places in sports, like Wrigley Field or Fenway Park. Near the end of the most glorious day he'd spent there, Keller called to an assistant, "Wait a minute," as the Delta team bus was about to pull away. Keller walked back inside, up the gritty steps, onto the main landing, and out to the edge of the court. And there he stood. The lights had been dimmed. The place was almost empty — a few people were cleaning up. He looked all around — at the brick wall at the stage end of the building, at the big Indian head in the center of the floor. He looked far up the rows of bleachers until they faded to darkness near the ceiling. Moments passed. Then he turned and walked back to the bus.

The regional at Hinkle Fieldhouse generated still another surprise. Indianapolis Cathedral, which had beaten Ben Davis in the morning, scored an unlikely parlay by upsetting North Central in the evening. On the same day Cathedral beat two top-ten teams, the supposed class of Indianapolis, both threats to win the state title. In a Sunday column in the *Indianapolis Star* Robin Miller said that Cathedral's sweep "defined the competitive spirit of Hoosier Hysteria."

North Central guard Jason Gardner finished his sophomore season with yet another excellent performance, scoring 25 points against Cathedral. Huggy Dye ended his one season in Indiana by shooting only two for ten to finish with six points. "The difference between Jason Gardner and Huggy Dye is in the box score," their coach, Doug Mitchell, said over breakfast a few mornings later. "But Huggy's a survivor. He'll be heard from." After North Central, he would enroll in prep school at Maine Central Institute.

In Gary, number eight Merrillville faced Gary West Side on its court. Jim East was well prepared, although he had been foiled in a strange way one time as he was about to scout Gary West Side. On February 20, during a bitter rain, a cloud of noxious fumes escaped from a chemical plant in Hammond, bringing the northwest corner of the state to a stop. The Indiana Toll Road and commuter rail lines shut down, causing late-afternoon and evening chaos. Among all the inconveniences, the Bishop Noll–Gary West Side game was canceled.

When Merrillville and Gary West Side finally got together in the regionals, the outcome could not have been more discouraging to East. Jamaal Davis and the four guards almost won. It took a couple of oddities near the end of the game for Gary West to prevail, 57–56. Two problems with the clock in the last 7.8 seconds cost Merrillville the game, as East viewed it. Gary West Side used the extra seconds to launch a desperation, winning three-pointer from 35 feet as time expired.

The end came for Merrillville just when East was beginning to think that his Pirates could make it past the regionals and into the semistate at Purdue. "When you get that far," he said, "anything can happen." As it actually happened, Merrillville vanished from the tournament with scant coverage downstate. It was as East had said in the beginning, teams from "The Region" could be easily dismissed in the rest of Indiana.

In the Coliseum at Fort Wayne, number seventeen DeKalb won as narrowly as Merrillville had lost. A game-ending play by Luke Recker lifted the Barons into the "sweet sixteen" with an upset of fourth-ranked Fort Wayne South Side, led by Cameron Stephens. Fort Wayne South Side had won 24 straight games. With 8.5 seconds left, Stephens hit a three-pointer to tie DeKalb at 52. But Recker took the inbounds pass, dribbled the length of the floor, and, as Stephens came out to meet him, fed big Shane Monroe running alongside for the game-winning layup. "What happened on that play was a result of what Luke had learned at the Hall of Fame Classic," DeKalb's Cliff Hawkins would say later. "In the Hall of Fame Classic he could have upped the ball to Nate Brown. Now he dishes to Monroe. The buzzer goes off. The DeKalb Barons are regional champions. Luke's first comment to a TV reporter was, 'Coach said a great player is one who gives it up.' He could have challenged Cameron. But instead of forcing the shot himself, he gave it up to Monroe. Beautiful."

Regional Saturday was over. It was close to midnight, traffic was light, the stars were out. Garry Donna of *Hoosier Basketball* magazine was on "Network Indiana" talking about Michael Menser and Batesville and the game he had witnessed back at New Castle. Donna had a poor phone connection, but from the excitement in his voice listeners could get his gist. Bob Lovell, the host, declared the entire day of regionals to have been remarkable. The two smallest schools had lost in other regionals, but not until both had won their openers and advanced to the evening championship games. Then Bloomington North, number one in the final coaches' poll, eliminated tiny Union, 62–51, and little Barr-Reeve fell to Pike Central, 39–37. It had been a day and a night of games to remember.

It was when Indiana high school basketball had been so riveting at the same time in so many places. When North Central and Ben Davis lost on the same day at Hinkle, when Anderson was upset and the Wigwam closed for the season, when Merrillville barely lost in Gary, and when DeKalb barely won in Fort Wayne. You know how memorable all those games had to have been, yet without doubt you'd make the same choice again — to be in New Castle, in the world's largest high school fieldhouse, when Batesville played for itself, and the Indiana ideal that the little team could do it, even though it didn't.

The following afternoon, Hecklinski was propped up in bed watching a North Carolina–North Carolina State game on television. He'd said little to Pam or Stephanie all that Sunday, but moped about the house, more dispirited than he'd been at any time during the season. He was supposed to be "running with the wind." He thumbed listlessly through the newspaper, sat in his chair in the den, went back to bed. He felt pretty much as he had after the end of every basketball season — achingly empty. But maybe not quite as empty. This ending did not seem as painful as all the other endings, when, he said, "I hurt so much it was like someone had whipped me and beat me up — and it took me a long, long time, a week, a week and a half, to get over it."

He was sitting in bed watching the players on the screen but thinking of the game that had ended Anderson's season, trying to put the end of a season into a perspective he never had before. *Man, I've been given an extended life,* he told himself. *What's a loss when I have my life?* A grown man might be expected to reach the right answer to such questions pretty quickly. But because he hated losing, because he was still competitive, he was grappling with his own questions when Stephanie came into the room and climbed up onto the bed next to him.

"Why do you look so upset?" she asked.

"Well, you know, Steph, the Indians lost. We got beat."

She looked up at him and said: "Dad, it's only a game. You're here with me. Dad, we start our softball next week. We've got to get out and play softball."

He pulled her close to him. "You're right, Steph," he said, "you're right. It's time for softball."

19

End of a Dream

A T 7:30 A.M., on the way north to the Fort Wayne semistate featuring DeKalb's Luke Recker, a caravan of cars came into view heading in the opposite direction. Delta's followers were on the move down I-69 from Muncie toward Indianapolis and the semistate at Hinkle Fieldhouse. A police escort, red lights flashing, cleared the route as other traffic gave way. The Delta cars were decorated in navy and gold, streamers flowing in the crisp morning air.

The Indiana high school basketball tournament was down to sixteen teams, playing at four locations. Two of the best, Bloomington North (24–1) and the 1996 runner-up New Albany, were in the Evansville semistate; New Castle (24–1) was the favorite at Hinkle; the semistates at Purdue and the Fort Wayne Coliseum were wide open. Recker was the most touted player still playing, having recently been named to the McDonald's All-

America team, a group of twenty-four seniors from around the country.

This late stage of the tournament had always been the occasion for a week of celebrations at the various schools, and drew the whole state together. In the glory days of 1928 through 1935 a sportswriter named Bill Fox and Tony Hinkle, who would become the coaching legend, would tour the sixteen schools in a Stutz Bearcat. The twofold purpose of the journey was publicity generated by Fox and the opportunity for Hinkle to scout out some of the best high school players for his Butler University teams. Hinkle would drive so that Fox could type his stories for the *Indianapolis News*; he wrote a column called "Shootin' 'em and Stoppin' 'em."

Fox's 1932 account begins, "One week from today they will be over — winter and the tournament — and spring will be here, mates, and a champion will have been crowned . . . as sweet as this blue and white songbird that has us humming over the highways to ye regional rajas. . . . Under skies of blue and a sweet shower of sunshine, over a snow blanket, we're off. . . ."

The week of the current semistates began somberly in Indianapolis. Roger Brown, the original of the Indiana Pacers of the American Basketball Association, died of cancer. An adopted Hoosier, he was mourned by more than a thousand people who filed quietly into Market Square Arena for a memorial service. After signing with the Pacers in 1967, Brown had gone on to become one of Indiana's most popular players. His casket was placed at center court, George McGinnis and other former and current Pacers were pallbearers.

Reminiscences of Brown's feats led off sportscasts that were dominated by basketball news: the sad standing of the present-day Pacers, updates on the NCAA tournament, with its finals to be held in Indianapolis, updates from the high school tournament, with all its upsets and most surprising school, Delta. Auburn's *Evening Star* printed the schedule when tickets would be sold at DeKalb for the Fort Wayne semistate. "Big Red ticket holders" and students got their chance on Tuesday, DeKalb County residents late Tuesday and Wednesday, and the general public on Thursday. "All persons except babes in arms must have a ticket for admittance," the paper said.

Fort Wayne was where two French journalists came in 1996 and 1997, somewhat like the Lynds to Muncie decades before, to study and report about a quintessential midwestern American city. The Fort Wayne Coliseum was home to the Fort Wayne Komets, a minor league hockey team, and the Continental Basketball Association's Fury — and Cliff Hawkins talked it up among his players as a "home" of the DeKalb Barons because of its proximity and the team's success there the previous week — beating Woodlan and Fort Wayne South Side for the regional title. "We played the first game and we were out of there before the tip of the second game," he said. "The players were back in their homes. No hotel. It was like a home game."

Recker's play, an effective zone-press defense, and just enough offense coaxed from the other players had made the difference for DeKalb in the regional. At the half of DeKalb's first game against Woodlan, Hawkins said, he psyched up six-six Shane Monroe, who had no points: "If we would lose this game, would you be able to say that you left it all out on the floor in terms of offensive play? I know you have no phone, but I have friends who belong to the FBI and they will haunt you for the rest of your life."

Monroe scored ten points in the second half and then 19 against Fort Wayne South Side, including the first nine points of the second half and the winning basket. Hawkins had implored Monroe to "exert" himself, which was what he was doing when running alongside Recker in the final seconds. The Barons were given a police escort home, and fire trucks led them through Auburn. Almost a thousand people were there when they walked into their gym at a little after 11 P.M.

"The close games we had during the season prepared us for the tournament, especially for Fort Wayne South Side," Recker said before a practice for the semistates. "We didn't panic when Cam Stephens hit that three-pointer. In our minds we knew what to do — just move the ball upcourt. The South Side players were celebrating a little bit. Cam was the only one who got back. All I kept thinking was pass, and then I saw Shane just standing there open. It was kind of a simple play."

Recker and Stephens had embraced at the end of the game, with Recker trying to cheer up Stephens, pointing out that they likely would play other important games against one another in college with Recker going to Indiana and Stephens to Purdue. Recker said that Stephens told him, "I want you to win state for me now. If I can't do it, there's no one I'd rather have do it than you."

The next evening Bob Knight phoned Recker at home and kidded him. Familiar with his sixty-one-shot debacle at the Hall of Fame Classic, Knight commended Recker by feigning surprise at his game-winning assist against Fort Wayne South Side, saying, "Sounds like you can pass, too."

As if taking the cue, Recker relied as much on his passing as his shooting in DeKalb's morning semistate game against Plymouth. Kokomo and East Noble would play the second game. Gray-bearded Clyde Lovellette, onetime star of Terre Haute Garfield, 1952 NCAA champion Kansas, and the Minneapolis Lakers, sat with long legs crossed a few rows behind a basket in the sold-out Coliseum. Another man who stood out in the crowd of 10,000 wore a T-shirt with a tombstone on the front and the inscription: "Hoosier Hysteria 1911–1997. It was ill so they called Commissioner Kavorcian [sic]"; and on the back, a vintage automobile with: "Class Basketball 1998, the Next Edsel."

In the fourth period of a 76–52 rout by DeKalb, Recker produced the most sensational play of the day — and one of the most spectacular seen all season. Moving along the baseline from the right corner, he raised his arm, calling for a pass. The alley-oop from Nate Brown landed on the palm of Recker's right hand but Recker already was climbing the front of teammate Monroe on the way to the basket. A defender also was sandwiched between them. In one unbroken stride Recker soared overtop both, turned his wrist, and flipped the ball off the glass and into the net. He finished with 27 points, 10 rebounds, and seven assists.

"It's remarkable how multitalented he is, how complete a basketball player he is," said Plymouth's coach, Jack Edison. "You don't guard him one-on-one. It takes help on him. But for people to see what a great passer he is, what an unselfish player he is. He got the ball through two or three times, they were just backbreakers. And" — with a smile — "they tell me he's not a halfway bad shooter either.

"But he handles the ball so well. And the thing that impressed us during the week as we watched him was his defense." Recker had stepped up his defense after the early losses. "The deflections — how much he takes away from your offense. Really, he's a complete player. I think I.U. really is looking at him to get the ball to people. He not only can, but he will. . . . He's so good. I think he's got a great heart, this kid does. I think he's got a lot of savvy. I think he's got the grit it takes.

"I think that's the only thing Knight wants to know. He just wants to know, are you a champion? Are you a winner on the inside? I can see your talent, but can you go through the discipline I'm going to throw at you? Can you go through everything we're going to put you through, the demanding practices, the demanding concentration it takes outside? If he's got that mental toughness — and I think he does — he'll be a factor early there."

A few hours later, however, Kokomo took Recker off his game — Recker and everyone else on the DeKalb team. Basil Mawbey, Indiana's master of the zone defense, was responsible. Kokomo used its two-three zone to stop East Noble, then in the evening game challenged DeKalb's shots both from in close and outside. Kokomo also sent its quick guards slicing through the middle of DeKalb's trapping defenses. The result: number fourteen Kokomo beat number seventeen DeKalb 69–46. Well before the final buzzer the DeKalb players wore the look of defeat. Recker's eyes looked glazed as he bent down, waiting for a free throw to be taken. Tears flowed in the DeKalb locker room; Recker had scored 21, but the team's 17-game winning streak and its season, 26–4, was over. Recker had averaged 26.8 points, 6.8 rebounds, 4.8 assists, and three steals. He'd scored 2,008 points, putting him in the top thirty of all-time Indiana high school scorers.

"Go ahead and cry a little bit," Hawkins told his players, who had gathered around him. Hawkins himself had trouble holding back the tears. "You don't ever know when it's going to end. But I love coaching you guys. I think we've done things the right way. You should be proud. You grow from everything that you go through. You do. A year ago we couldn't win the regional. Now we won the regional. We won the first game of the semistate. We just couldn't quite go on, we couldn't quite go on. Daggonit. I know right now those tears are real because when something ends it hurts. But it always makes you stronger and you go on to the next thing in life and that is how we're going to be successful as people. You've done so much winning for DeKalb it's unbeliev-able. Think of how much fun we had playing basketball the Baron way."

Recker moved from player to player, speaking as he made his way around the room: "I've had a lot of fun with you guys. You guys are like my family. Every day at practice, it was so much fun this year. Everybody. The managers, all you guys." He was choked up and paused.

One of the student managers, Tom Rudolph, broke the silence. From across the room he looked up from the bench he was sitting on and said softly to Recker: "Thanks for the ride, man."

"Thank you," said Recker.

A bank of television cameras and line of interviewers awaited Recker on the edge of the court. Showered and dressed, he went through each one. It wasn't easy. He kept his emotions in check as he commended Kokomo — "That's probably the best two-three zone you're going to see in high school basketball" — and described his own feelings: "It's really tough. It's sad to remember ending my high school career on this, but at the same time I've got to look back and know it was a heck of a run, I had a good four years. We're not champions on the scoreboard, but deep down we're champions in our hearts. We did our best. Everything I'll remember from DeKalb is going to be a sweet memory."

When he'd finished, Recker's sisters, who were nearby, gathered around him and then he climbed into the stands, where his mother was standing, several rows up. Marti hugged him and he began to cry again. And then he climbed higher in the stands to where his father was, leaning on a railing. Luke put his head on Clair Recker's shoulder. "I told him, 'I know how you feel,'" said Clair Recker. "'You were great. You were great all year. You were great your whole career.' I couldn't have been more proud of him. I really believe talent-wise we could have beat them. It was one of those things. It had been Luke's dream to win the state championship. It had been one of the things he had hoped for. If he didn't say it, I know he was thinking it. It was a sad ending."

At length it was time for the DeKalb players to leave. Recker caught up with his teammates, signed autographs as he crossed a Coliseum lobby toward vans waiting outside with their motors running.

Basil Mawbey walked across the lobby last. He was alone, carrying the game ball, smiling. "Took a few defeats to get this," he said to no one in particular.

It was close to midnight on the road back to Indianapolis when a caravan of cars came into view, heading in the opposite direction. Delta's followers were on the move north on I-69, toward Muncie and home. A police escort, red lights flashing, cleared the way. Delta had won two games at Hinkle Fieldhouse and advanced still further in the tournament, to the following Saturday's final four.

20

The Final
Final Four

T HE PEOPLE'S choice was quickly obvious as Indianapolis's RCA Dome filled for the high school tournament's last day. Delta was the smallest school — 916 students to Kokomo's 2,037, LaPorte's 1,861, and Bloomington North's 1,245. Judging from the roar of the crowd of 27,843, fourth largest to see an Indiana high school basketball game, Delta was the sentimental choice for a sentimental event, the final final four as Indiana had known it since 1911.

Delta was the one finalist that would not be a Class 4A school in 1997–98. It would be in the next group, 3A, but that was small enough to give the majority in the crowd a team to cheer for, and a long-gone time to dream about. Among the dreamers were Milan's 1954 players, watching from a mezzanine box. They get together at least once a year — this was their forty-third annual reunion.

Eight of the ten from '54 were there, most still living in Indiana:

Plump; Ray Craft, the IHSAA associate director; Gene White, head of the math department at Franklin High; Glen Butte, retired athletic director at Batesville; Rollin Cutter, guidance counselor at Noblesville High; Roger Schroeder, retired high school coach; Ken Wendleman, owner of a construction company in Versailles; and Bob Engel, who worked in the maintenance department at a General Motors plant in Kalamazoo, Michigan. (Bill Jordan lived in California; Ronnie Truitt had died.)

"It was a team in the truest sense," said Engel. "There never was any jealousy. Since then, there's never been a time when we haven't been there for each other."

"We weren't the best basketball players who ever played," said White. "We are the best team that ever played, taking the true meaning of the word *team* as sort of family."

What could be said of Milan's 1954 team could be said of Delta in 1997: this was a team that made few mistakes. If there was one explanation for Delta's success it was that the guards rarely turned the ball over. Delta excelled not because of height — the center was six one, flanked by two six-three forwards. It had good team speed, a speedy scoring guard in Patrick Jackson, and well-executed play. Keller, the coach, said he liked to divide the game into four-minute intervals and see where the team was — and where it had been over the previous two weeks was out in front of bigger schools.

Keller said he and the players had dedicated their final-four appearance to "all the men who have played [Delaware] county basketball but came up a little bit short."

The other three teams had their appeal: top-ranked Bloomington North, with its multinational makeup; LaPorte, which hadn't been to the final four since 1944; and Kokomo, which had in Basil Mawbey a feisty coach who could win close games and who had guided Connersville to the state title in 1983, by a point. He was one of those Indiana coaches who'd moved around in his twenty-seven years, with Delta among his five stops. Joe Otis, who had spent his entire seventeen years of coaching at LaPorte, summed up people's feelings about the tournament: "This is a rich, vibrant tradition that, no matter how you repackage, will never be the same."

It was 10:35 A.M., the crowd was in place for Kokomo versus Bloomington North. For a half, Kokomo played its game, keeping the score low, leading 20–16. But in the second half Bloomington North's big Kueth Duany and Djibril Kante, both juniors, took control and Bloomington North advanced to the final, 50–43.

The 12:30 game was the exciting one. Delta saw to it. LaPorte got off to a 20–9 lead, but Delta fought back the entire game. With 34 seconds remaining LaPorte led 56–55. With 9.7 seconds left and time called, Keller worked up a play. Delta's cheerleaders chanted "We believe," and noise filled the huge space beneath the white bubble roof. The play worked: Jackson fed Tyce Shideler, a six-three forward, for a layup. Final: 57–56, Delta.

LaPorte's Otis, a history teacher, took defeat with composure: "First of all, I want to thank my high school coach, Virgil Sweet, for bringing me here thirty years ago. I was just a kid then, fifteen years old, and it was exciting for me. And I still have this kid's love for the great game of basketball. I want to thank all my teachers for giving me a poet's appreciation of its beauty, and particularly this tournament. You know, this is the end of the single-class tournament, and part of its attractiveness is the Shakespearean element, I guess, to endings. Like what happened to us today."

The crowd refilled the arena in the evening for Indiana's eighty-seventh state championship game, most there to root for Delta. They were dreaming. Bloomington North was the last true champion, and proved it from beginning to end. It wasn't close, 75–54. Bloomington North finished its season 28–1, that lone defeat suffered in overtime on a January Saturday night in the Wigwam. Keller told his players: "Hold your heads up like winners." What else was there to do? As Gene White of the 1954 Milan team said: "David doesn't beat Goliath very often, that's why it's still a good story."

21

Later

ON APRIL 8, 1997, the Indiana High School Athletic Association reversed itself, after a fashion. Indiana would have a single champion after all, at least a compromise single champion. Pressure from state legislators prompted the IHSAA to set up a "tournament of champions" in which the four class champions would meet in one final Saturday showdown. Predictably, people still were unhappy — and for good reason.

"They took the wimpy way out," said Lafayette Jeff coach Jim Hammel, observing that three of the four teams that had won class championships certainly weren't going to feel like "champions" when they lost during the tacked-on weekend of play.

"I'm really confused," said Ben Davis's Steve Witty, though he really wasn't. "Why did they all of a sudden change their minds? When they voted to go to the multi-class tournament, they voted against the four champions meeting each other. And now they decide to go back and change it. If we're going back to having one champion, then why did we go away from the original tournament anyway?''

A political organization, the IHSAA had collided with a bigger political organization — the Indiana General Assembly. In a news release, the IHSAA admitted that legislators had threatened steps that would establish a new organization to run Indiana high school athletics.

"Members of the Indiana General Assembly have made several attempts to pass legislation that would intervene in the structure of the newly adopted multiple class basketball tournament and the governance structure of the IHSAA. In addition, there was support most recently for a legislative attempt to create a new organization to regulate high school athletics governed by a seven-member board elected by the general public. A similar challenge appeared likely during the 1998 legislative session."

Bob Gardner, the IHSAA commissioner, said the compromise "tournament of champions" would be in effect for a two-year trial, just as the multi-class system would be. The compromise was reached, he added, after meetings among the IHSAA board and various legislators who opposed multi-class basketball. "It is the consensus of the leadership of the IHSAA that this is the best course of action to bring closure to this issue with the Indiana General Assembly," said Gardner. The IHSAA vote was 11–0.

"I still think the old way was the best," Larry Bird said. "If you had the opportunity to work your way through the tournament, every step would get bigger and bigger. That way, when a small school got to play the big boys the small school was ready. This way, you haven't been prepared for that.

"If things ain't broke you shouldn't fix 'em — that's how I feel. And I don't feel they were broken. Usually, the people who make the decisions haven't played the game."

Bobby Plump was happy enough, for the moment. "It's better

than what we had a week ago," he said. "Is it what I really wanted? No." But he had new hope that in two years either public demand or pressure from the legislature would persuade the IHSAA to reverse itself completely and return to the original single-class system — although others believed the IHSAA simply was buying time and hoping the issue would die. Plump's shot, as it were, hit the rim and, judging from the scramble still going on, was still in play.

Following the IHSAA board's action, the Indiana House of Representatives approved a resolution supporting the plan by voice vote.

"The resolution has passed," declared House Speaker John Gregg of Sandborn. "The republic has been saved."

Anderson. Eric Bush, after conferring with Gary Weatherford, decided he did not want to commit to Purdue, preferring to demonstrate his abilities in front of an array of college coaches at the Nike summer camp in Indianapolis. "I think Eric's done the right thing," Hecklinski said. "There's no sense in rushing. Look, I've been on the other side as a college assistant. Eric's a great talent. He plays the game all-out. He's growing physically stronger, and I see him growing mentally stronger as a person. He's got a great career ahead of him. He's going to be all right."

Weatherford still faced a court date as the result of his arrest. But three Anderson police officers were disciplined with either brief suspensions from the force or a reprimand. The action came three days after an editorial in Anderson's *Herald-Bulletin* criticizing the police for the way they handled the arrest and the length of time, a month, that its internal investigation was taking. The paper's editorial said: "The case hardly called for Weatherford to be hauled out of the Wigwam in handcuffs before a near-capacity crowd."

Bush's father, Charles Bush, lost his night job and apartment. He became a welder, but his future remained uncertain.

Hecklinski was retained as Anderson's coach when the city's three high school staffs were reduced to two. His hernia surgery was successful — but for a few days the pain was excruciating. Scar tissue that had built up on his stomach muscle was scraped away. "I feel worse than I did after the transplant," he said a few days later. But it was nothing in comparison; he already was back at home in his easy chair, moving only when he had to. "I've used up two lives," he said. "I got seven to go." Later, he endured headaches and nausea as steroid treatment was lessened.

DeKalb. Luke Recker overwhelmingly won the Indiana high schools' most prestigious individual award, "Mr. Basketball." He received 142½ votes of coaches and media. Batesville's Michael Menser was second, with 66. Fort Wayne South Side's Cameron Stephens was third, with 41½. The remaining 64 votes were shared by 21 players. Recker played in several postseason all-star games, including the McDonald's All-America game in Colorado and an all-star doubleheader at South Bend. "Luke's approach to the game was more than expected," said Batesville's Melvin Siefert, who coached one of the teams at South Bend. "His grandfather was seriously ill and he had to miss one practice. Yet he managed to get there for the second day of practice. He's a very, very impressive kid." Recker would wear the coveted "No. 1" for the Indiana all-stars in their traditional two-game series with the Kentucky all-stars and, after a month more of weightlifting and some relaxed shooting, would report to Bloomington for his initiation under Knight.

Merrillville. After Jamaal Davis turned in an excellent season — averaging 18.2 points, 8.8 rebounds, and 4.5 blocks — he showed signs of discouragement, according to his coach, Jim East. Davis received only eight votes for "Mr. Basketball." His play in an Indiana north-south all-star game at Batesville was lackadaisical, according to several coaches. "He didn't have a lot of enthusiasm and intensity about him," a coach said. "I would have thought that it was the time to be enthusiastic and interested."

Davis, nevertheless, was named to the roster of the Indiana all-star team that would play the Kentucky all-stars — but not before an all-star team official phoned East to ask if Davis really wanted to play. "I think he managed to make the team on the basis of his whole career," East said. "He seems to have other things on his mind."

But in May, East related that he and Davis had discussed the player's future at length. "His attitude is improved," said East. "I'm hopeful. He's a likable kid. He's been perceived as a rebel. There's a certain rebelliousness to him. But I've always liked Jamaal. I can't say that about every player I've coached. Jamaal has a great feel for the game. He can go out and shoot from the perimeter. He has great hands. He can put the ball on the floor. He can pass. His timing on blocked shots is great — he rarely fouls. He can be a tremendous talent." But Davis would not get to show that talent for the Indiana all-stars.

On Wednesday morning June 11 he was involved in a serious automobile accident on I-65 while returning home from a visit to Purdue. State police said Davis was driving erratically and at an "excessively high rate of speed" when he apparently lost control of his Chevrolet Blazer in a construction zone. The truck veered into a grassy median and flipped at least once, and Davis was thrown from the vehicle. The Blazer reportedly careened into a southbound lane in the work area and collided with a car driven by an Illinois man, who was said to suffer head trauma, a broken neck, and a skull fracture.

"He's lucky to be alive," said East after visiting Davis in the hospital. Davis suffered broken ribs, a bruised heart, and cuts. Remarkably, he was released from the hospital within days. In late July, though hardly in form, he played in an all-star game in Fort Wayne.

But police charged Davis with several violations in connection with the accident. Meanwhile, Davis said that the accident was caused by a double tire blowout. He faced a court date.

A Purdue spokesman said that Davis was scheduled to enroll at the university, but as far as basketball, he was a "Prop 48," meaning he would have to sit out his first college season until he became academically eligible to play.

Batesville. Michael Menser was surprised when Sherman Dillard, the college coach who had recruited him, left Indiana State to take the head coaching job at his alma mater, James Madison, in Virginia. In such a case the prospect has the option of not accepting his scholarship and going elsewhere, although he would lose one season of eligibility. Menser still wanted to go to Indiana State, and after meeting with Dillard's replacement, Royce Waltman, from a successful Division II program at the University of Indianapolis, Menser would be on his way to Terre Haute to play for the Sycamores.

Among letters that Menser received after the season was one addressed to "Mike Menser, #5." Milan coach Randy Combs wrote:

> I wanted to drop you a short note to congratulate you on your outstanding season and career. You represent the "essence" of an Indiana Basketball Player because of your commitment to your team, school, community, and the game itself. It was not as painful to lose to this Batesville team because in doing so, we knew that we had lost to a team that had earned its success through hard work and a commitment to each other. . . . The efforts of your team touched many in a positive way and the great memories will never die.

Over the course of my coaching career, I visualize myself using the example of Michael Menser and the Batesville Bulldogs as a model to emulate. Today in Batesville and in other southeastern Indiana communities, there is a young guard working on his game in his backyard so he can someday play like Michael Menser.

Parts of Indiana seem fixed in time: a solitary farmboy with a buzz haircut shooting a basketball at a milk carton affixed to a pole, a South Side Indy kid lifting high off the macadam in a serious pickup game. Many days, near dusk, a CSX freight still rumbles slowly through Milan, past the water tower painted in tribute to the 1954 state high school basketball champions. And yet many Hoosiers say their game may never be the same.

Change has swept through Indiana and taken with it one of the state's best-loved traditions. The realization that single-class basketball and its tournament have vanished is a truth better known after spending a season in Indiana. Batesville coach Melvin Siefert says, "I hope that somehow we can get back to the old way."

Until then, Hoosiers still will fill the gyms and Indiana kids will keep shooting basketballs, and ultimately some still will become legends. Unswervingly positive, Hoosiers may be content knowing they're on the side of the angels and their sainted spokesman for basketball, John Wooden, Martinsville High, class of '28. In Indiana he's still called Johnny.

"Although there is no progress without change, all change is not progress," Wooden said. "A change to class basketball in Indiana high school tournament play would not be progress. More doesn't mean better. Nor does bigger. The Indiana state basketball tournament is easily the equivalent of the NCAA tournament and is more highly regarded than the tournaments in any other state. As Cervantes said, 'The journey is better than the inn.'"